THE COURAGE TO STAND

We live in a culture today, where Christians/Church needs *The Courage to Stand!* Too many Christians/Churches need to arise, and be Spirit-filled, Spirit-baptized and Spirit-empowered to live a life of courage today.

Marsha Mansour has a purpose and passion to call the "Church" to arise and be all that God has called us to in this world. As Marsha's pastor and friend, I highly recommend to you her newest book, "The Courage To Stand." This is a book for every leader and every follower of Jesus to arise and be all that God has called us to be today.

Christians and the church must rise in courage, and not back down, or retreat, because of everything that is going on in our culture today. When the world is at its worst, the church must be at its best. This is true today; we must have the courage to rise up!

Marsha will inspire and instruct us on how we can have the courage to stand up. Marsha lives this out in her daily life and her ministry as a Revivalist as she travels to all kinds of churches.

I highly recommend this book and recommend that you invite Marsha to come and minister in your church.

—Ronald Squibb, Lead Pastor
International Christian Center, Staten Island, NY

*　*　*

"For such a time as this!" In these crazy times that we live in, God has raised up a voice to call the Church to be the Church. Marsha Mansour is a bold woman of faith that is using her "platform" all around the world. She teaches and urges believers to live in the supernatural and to uphold the highest biblical standards (in the face of such evil). Her message is Christ-centered, Holy Ghost inspired, and rooted in prayer. Marsha moves in the gifts of prophecy, healing, and deliverance. She is deeply concerned for the future of our youth and the condition of anemic believers in the church. When you meet Marsha Mansour, you have a friend for life because she sincerely cares about YOU.

—Chris & Julie Abiuso, Missionaries in Mexico

THE COURAGE TO
STAND

THE COURAGE TO
STAND
REMNANT CHURCH RISE

MARSHA MANSOUR

CONTENTS

INTRODUCTION

The Lord spoke to me and said, "Allow Me to use you as an igniter to My Church and awaken My bride. It is time to be My Church. It is time to wake up." I answered, "Yes, God." Essentially, God was asking me not just to pastor one church but to help Him pastor the Church at large.

To better understand what God was saying to me, we must look at the church that Jesus built. Jesus built the church we see in the Book of Acts. That church was built on His testimony, His resurrection, and the power of the Holy Spirit. That church had power; that church was anointed and unapologetic about who she was. Those early followers had courage, boldness, and fearlessness. If we are honest, the pre-pandemic church in America did not look anything like the early church. The pre-pandemic church was built by man and looked nothing like the church Jesus built. We need to realize that God never asked us to build His church. Jesus said, in Matthew 16:18, "I will build my Church." We get the privilege to walk beside Him as He builds it, but he never intended for us to take over.

Yet, somehow the church of America grabbed hold of it and said *We are going to build it, and we are going to make it pretty. We are going to make it sound nice, look nice and make it socially acceptable.* And the church that Jesus built began to fade, going further and further away from what it was intended to be. We took the reins of the church and began to tell Jesus how to build His house. We tell the Holy Spirit, *You have five minutes in the service, so we would appreciate it if you could do whatever you are planning between the announcements and the preaching; we have an agenda to keep.* Can you imagine somebody coming to your house and telling you what to do in your own house?

Yet that is what we do to God. We put Him behind us, take the reins and say, *this is our church, and we want to do it our way.* However, we need to understand that Jesus gave us a clear mission. He said, "Go make disciples." That was His mission statement. Go make disciples. Nonetheless, we changed that mission statement to *fill the house.* At all costs, we must fill the house. Why? Because our success is no longer determined by the presence of the Holy Spirit but rather by the appearance of a fully occupied church. And so, we stopped making disciples and began making consumers.

Now, in order to fulfill our new mission statement, we changed the message. This new mission statement will not attract people who want to be challenged; therefore, we changed the message because the purpose has shifted. So we began by softening the message. We stopped talking about holiness; we stopped talking about sin; we stopped talking about repentance; and we stopped telling people that they are not allowed to sleep together before marriage. We stopped saying these things because people might get offended and leave our building.

So now we have a new mission statement. Can you guess what happened next? The power left; why? Because we serve a Holy God. The power walked out, and now attending church has essentially become a feel-good day. Come in for a good therapy session. Come in, hear some nice music and feel better. You may actually feel better, but you are not transformed.

The message went from, "Come as you are" to "Stay as you are." However, the true message will always be, "Come as you are." Walk in the door anyway that you are; broken, sinful, destroyed; but walk in. That is where your journey begins, and you will be challenged to change daily; why? Because we love you enough to tell you the truth, we want to see you transformed and become the Remnant people God has called us to be.

His servant,
Reverand Marsha Mofid Mansour
Founder of Marsha Mansour Ministries

THE COURAGE TO
STAND
REMNANT CHURCH RISE

THE REMNANT MUST RISE

In January 2020, I resigned from my pastoral position in New Jersey. I had been pastoring at that particular church for over fifteen years and pastoring overall for over two and a half decades. Towards the end of my time at that church, I began to feel a fresh calling from God to leave it all and become a full-time Revivalist. In obedience to the Lord, I resigned and did just that., That decision meant that my whole life, calling, and finances would depend solely on the Lord. Three months after resigning, COVID-19 appeared and began the infamous global pandemic that shut the world down. While this surprised many, God was not caught off guard and already knew this would happen. However, when you say *Yes* to God and where He is calling you, He promises to take care of all the details (even during a global pandemic). During this time, God was faithful to His Word; He took care of me and has faithfully continued to care for me ever since.

When the world shut down, I asked God, "Okay, now what? What's the plan?" God spoke and answered, "Teach my people how to pray. They need to learn how to elevate their prayers. Prayer 101 is not working anymore; they need to learn to pray at levels 102 and 103." My immediate response to hearing this was to start an online prayer meeting as a branch of my ministry. Shortly after, I announced that I would begin weekly prayer sessions, and a group of faithful people joined every Monday evening. As the group grew, we introduced another prayer session to the week and started praying every Monday and Thursday evening. This group of faithful prayer warriors continued to grow, and we now have people from around the world praying with us and have seen God do unbelievable miracles through this online prayer meeting. We have seen people healed from fibromyalgia, lupus, cancer, COVID-19, pain, and many other illnesses. We are still praying to this day and will continue to pray until Jesus says otherwise.

One night during a prayer meeting, we had an unsaved woman join who was encouraged by a friend to tune in. Later that night, she made the decision to give her heart to the Lord and even was baptized in the Holy Spirit. As the night continued, she revealed that she was in a wheelchair due to the severity of her sciatic pain. I prayed for her at that moment, and God instantly healed her back. She no longer needed her wheelchair; she went to sleep that night pain-free. The next morning, her unsaved family rang the doorbell, and she got up and ran to answer the door! When her family saw her, their response was, "What are you doing?" And as she started jumping, they asked, "What happened?" She told them, "Jesus happened! Jesus happened!"

The above story is just one example of many miraculous stories that occur during our prayer meetings. A woman who had nodules on her lungs has been healed; another woman had COVID-19 and has been healed. The testimonies go on and on. God has provided a tremendous opportunity to build an online prayer meeting with thousands of believers from all over the country and the world. I see people from Poland, France, and Canada who stay up at night for the opportunity to pray with us. Anyone can join by using our app, Facebook, or Youtube page. We have seen God use this prayer meeting powerfully amid a pandemic. During the shutdown, I heard the Lord say, "Don't worry; my Spirit transcends everything."

Can I tell you, family, I am so excited about a time like this! You may say, "How in the world can she be excited for a time like this? Can't she see what is happening?" I know we live in "unprecedented times," but the Church must learn to look through the lens of the Spirit. Instead, we should say, "we live in prophetic times." That is why I am so excited. In just a short time, we have jumped 50 years. We are no longer *reading* the Book of Revelation; we are *living* in the Book of Revelation. We are no longer *reading* the book of Daniel or 1st Peter; we are *living* them. We have entered the last days.

Let me share some information for those who question whether we are living in the last days. I am an Egyptian woman born in the Middle East, and I have witnessed Israel and Saudi Arabia sit down together to sign a peace treaty; this alone is a sign that we are living in prophetic times. A peace treaty between those two countries was unheard of in the past. These two groups of people had such hatred towards each other, yet they sat down and signed a treaty. It is just as the Book of Revelation says. We are truly living in prophetic times, and that makes me excited. I'm excited because I've already finished the Book and know how the story ends. I know how dark it will become, but I also know that King Jesus wins! No matter what happens, the Kingdom of Jesus Christ wins, we win, and the Household of Faith wins. This moment is what we can call an Esther moment, "For such a time as this," and I feel privileged and honored that God, Himself, would allow me to live in such a time as this. I repeat, for you to live during this time is a true honor and privilege. It is an expression of God's trust in you. There is a great mantle on the Church of Jesus Christ. The word mantle literally means a weight of responsibility has been placed upon you. There is a weight and a mantle on the Church, and it is the same mantle that was on Jesus. As Jesus ascended to Heaven, He turned around and said, "Now you finish what I started."

The mantle is simply this: Advance the Kingdom of Jesus Christ, advance the Gospel of Jesus Christ, and preach the Word. Yet somehow, the Church is confused when it comes to this mantle. Suddenly, we think we have a different mission. We think we should focus our efforts elsewhere, but there is no other job. The mantle is the mantle, and it is the job and purpose of the Church of Jesus Christ. We do not have a new job description. Our job description stays the same no matter the season. Let me make this clear, the only hope for the world is the True Church of Jesus Christ. Without the Kingdom, the world is doomed. We are the hope of the world; without us, the world is doomed. We can't afford to be confused and think that we have a different purpose other than the true purpose given to us by God. Our purpose is simple: Advance the Kingdom of Jesus Christ, advance the Gospel of Jesus Christ, and preach the Word.

A while back, I saw a post by a minister whom I think highly of, who said, "The Church cannot hide behind the preaching of the Gospel to handle the racial issues in our country." I immediately read it twice because I did not want to misunderstand it. While I love this brother, I want to tell you that he is wrong, dead wrong. The only answer for the racial problems in our country is the Gospel. In fact, the only answer for any issues in our country, lives and politics is the Gospel. The Gospel is the only answer for anything going on, and there is no other answer. What this minister's statement proposed is that the cross is not enough. Somehow we have made the cross insufficient. But the truth is that the cross is more than enough. It is Jesus, plus nothing equals everything!

The second we think we need something else is the moment we have changed the Gospel and, by default, altered our job. Jesus did not shy away from racial issues but met them head-on. Look at John 4, when Jesus met the woman at the well. Talk about division! Jesus walked right up to her, and she called him a Jew, "You are a Jew." He listened, she talked, and at the conclusion of their conversation, she said, "You are the Savior of the world!" What happened to her initial response of, "You are a Jew!" I'll tell you what happened, she was met with the Gospel, and any racial barrier was instantly broken. Jesus did not shy away from controversy but walked right up to it because He knew He was sufficient; He was enough. And now, all of a sudden, many feel that we must find a different way to do what we know to do. Brothers and sisters, there is only one way, there is only one Kingdom, and there is only one Word to preach, and it is the Gospel of Jesus Christ.

You may ask, *"So what happened to this minister you thought so highly of?"* What happened is something that Jesus warned us about a long time ago. Luke 21 tells us that Jesus was walking with his disciples, and as he came up to Jerusalem, He began speaking prophetically to them. Jesus says to them, "You see the temple? There is coming a time when not one brick will be left upon another." Here Jesus is talking about the end times; the disciples then turn to Jesus and say, "Tell us when this time is." The reason they want to know is that they want to be ready. They want to prepare and possibly put food or money aside; however, the disciples are unsure of what they need. Jesus here does not answer their question; instead, He responds with, "Take heed that you are not deceived." Their biggest problem had nothing to do with physical preparation; their biggest problem was the possibility of being deceived. "Take heed that you are not deceived. For many will come in My name, saying 'I am He.'" Jesus told them not to worry about getting physically ready but to take heed and not be deceived. The minister I mentioned earlier was sadly deceived, and that is happening across the world – many are being deceived.

This is what God says, and it's the same advice God gave Joshua. "Don't look to the right or to the left. Look forward." Do you know how many times He tells that to Joshua? At least 22 times! Why? Because by nature, we look this way, and we look that way, but God said, "Take heed that you are not deceived," Many will rise and say, *This is what the Church needs to do*, and *That is what the Church needs to do*. I am telling you right now, Jesus has already given us our job description. Jesus has already told us what to do. We do not need a new job description; the cross will always be sufficient.

In the summer of 2020, I saw a post on my social media feed from a major mainstream denomination announcing that they would now acknowledge and support same-sex unions. At that moment, when they made that announcement, that entire denomination was deceived. They yielded to culture. They yielded to emotion; they yielded to the demands of man and turned from the Word of God. At that moment, they flipped the switch. As I watched this,

I heard the Holy Spirit prophetically speak to me, and He said, "There's no longer going to be a line in the sand. From this day forward, there will be a line in cement. It will be a clear line right in the middle of the cement. And at the end, only two churches will be left. No more than that, just two. One is an itchy-ear, culture-driven, emotionally-charged corrupt church, and the other is the Remnant. That is what will be left."

There is this itchy-ear, culture-driven, emotionally-charged corrupt church, and there is the Remnant of God. The word Remnant is defined as those that remain. Remain what? Grounded. Those that remain grounded, those that remain surrendered, those that remain true. We are already beginning to see the corrupt, itchy-ear, culture-driven, emotionally-charged churches where emotion trumps truth. They are based on the idea that *feelings* are more important than God's Word. They believe in chasing and following cultural demands. We have been called to lead the lost; however, we are led by the lost when the Church follows culture. Itchy ear literally means scratch my ears. *Don't tell me what I need to hear; tell me what I want to hear. Tell me what feels good and that I'm okay. Tell me that everything is wonderful and that I can make my own choices. Tell me that I'm right.* Can I tell you something? You do not love anyone if you tell them everything is okay and ignore the truth.

Love tells you the truth. But these itchy-ear Gospel people get offended quickly when you tell them the truth. They do not want to hear the truth because it offends them. Do you know what it really does? It convicts them. But they don't know the difference yet. This itchy-ear church is rising, demanding the Church to bend to culture. It demands the Church to bend to emotion and

9

demands that the people of God follow in the direction that the world is going.

The Church will burn that way because it was never intended to bend to culture. The Church was meant to lead the way. As a revivalist, God has called me specifically to remind the Church of who they are. We are the Church of Jesus Christ. We have the power and the anointing of the Spirit of God, and we are meant to lead, not follow. We are meant to tell people how to walk after God. Unfortunately, a corrupt church is rising and seeking to place its emotions over the Word of God. When I talk to people and quote scripture, they respond with, *I believe the Word, but I just don't agree with it. I just don't feel that's right,* or *that hurts my feelings, Pastor. You're offending me.* And I say to them, "Get over it, get over it. Grow up… grow up." Why? "Because we have work to do, and I need to ensure you are alright. What you are doing is sin." Their immediate response is, "Oh, no, Pastor. It's just a bad choice." But it's not; it's a sin. Yes, I am going to call it sin. Why? Because I love them, and if they hate me for loving them, that is their decision. I will not let their emotions or opinions trump the Word of God.

A corrupt church may be rising up but right beside it are the Remnant people. They might not be the most polished or visibly appealing, and they may even have dirt under their nails because they have been in the trenches with God, but they are rising up. They have remained true and continue to remain true. They focus on holding tight to His Word, His truth, and His Spirit. They yield, surrender and walk in righteousness and continuously pursue His glory. When the Zealots came to Jesus, they wanted Him to fight alongside them against the Romans; however, Jesus answered, "You don't know what kingdom I am trying to advance. I am not trying to advance the Jewish kingdom. I am trying to advance my Father's Kingdom." Our alliance is with the Lord, and our job is to advance His Kingdom. The Remnant people are rising up to advance His Kingdom. They hold fast to His Word, and they are about to see the greatest move of the Spirit of God in our lifetime. Revival is the power of God that changes lives; it is miraculous, it is a great conviction, it is anointing, and the Remnant are about to see Revival!

You may ask, *How does she know?* I know because the world has gone crazy, and if we look at the history of the Word of God, God's response to *crazy* is revival. Read about any revival story in history, and you'll see a world in turmoil succeeded by God showing up with power. The Remnant people are right on the crux of what God wants to do in His Church. With every church I visit, I feel the Spirit of God opening the heavens just a little, like God is getting ready to send a full rain. A full rain is coming, and we are on the threshold of a great move of God. There will be a clear distinction in the body of Christ, and every *believer* will have to choose.

Matthew 13 gives us great insight into the last days. Take a look at Matthew 13:24; here, Jesus tells a parable, "The Kingdom of Heaven is like a man who sowed good seed in his field. But while he slept, his enemy came and sowed tares among the wheat and went his way. But when the grain sprouted and produced a crop, the tares also appeared. So the servants of the owner came and said to him, 'Sir, did you not sow good seed in the field? How then does it have tares?' He said to them, 'An enemy has done this.' The servants then asked, 'Do you want us then to go and gather them up?' But he answered, 'No, lest while you gather up the tares you also uproot the wheat with them. Let both grow together until the harvest, and at the time of harvest I will say to the reapers, "First gather together the tares and bind them in bundles to burn, but gather the wheat into my barn." Jesus is telling the story of a man who owns a field of good soil. Soil, in this parable, is an image of our hearts. The man's soil was good, and he planted good seeds, specifically wheat. But while he was sleeping, an enemy came and planted tares among the good soil. Tare is another word for a weed, and while it may look very similar to wheat, it is still a weed. When the crop started to sprout, the servant noticed and asked the owner, "Did you not plant just wheat? What is this?" The owner replied, "An enemy has come and has planted weeds." The servants then wanted to know if they should rip them up, but the owner responded, "No, they look too similar. If you rip them up, you are going to also take good wheat. Leave them alone. Wait until harvest time. When harvest time comes, you will be able to distinguish them more easily. Then take the tares out first, bundle them and throw them into the fire. Then take the wheat, pull it out and bring it into my barn."

This story is significant because Jesus tells you exactly the message I am trying to bring you today. There will be two types of people left, just as there were two types of plants. In the parable, there is a new crop coming, but it is not obvious what the crop is because it is not harvest time, and since it's not harvest time, nothing needs to be done yet. Everything is wonderful when there is no pressure. Everything is great when nothing goes wrong, but harvest time will come, and the wheat and the tares will show themselves.

The tares always stand tall and stiff, full of pride when fully grown. These tares represent the itchy-ear, culture-driven, emotionally charged, corrupt church. Stiff and proud. But the Remnant, the wheat, will always bow when fully grown. What does this mean? They are always surrendered and yielded to the Lord. They are always bent over in obedience. The tares stand nice, tall, and arrogant and demand God's Word to bend. It is not that they do not use the Word, but about their positioning regarding the Word. They use the Word, but their hearts are not positioned to learn from it; instead, they are there to challenge and manipulate it. Let me tell you something, you can make this Word say anything you want. Pick out a verse, a line, a story, and you can make it say anything you want— And that is what the itchy-ear church does. They go to the Word, discount it and manipulate it. They make it satisfy what they want it to say. They say, *Well, God really did not mean that.* or, *Well, that was a long time ago. That does not apply to me. Maybe the author got it wrong. Maybe the translation is messed up.* and so they manipulate the Word of God.

The Remnant Church positions itself under the Word, not over it. What The Word says is final. If God calls it sin, I call it sin. If He loves it, I love it. If He hates it, I hate it. The Remnant church yields not just to some things but to everything. They yield their emotions and convictions while the itchy-ear church stiffens up, and their emotions take precedence. What they feel takes precedence, "Well, I don't agree with that in the Word of God, so I'm not going to use it, 'I feel differently about it." Chapter 17 in the Book of Jeremiah tells us something very clearly. It tells us that the evilest thing we own is our emotions. Our emotions are the most wicked thing in our body; they will deceive and destroy us. Following anything besides the Word of God in complete obedience, will deceive you. That is why Jesus said, "Take heed that you are not deceived." Why? Because it is possible to be deceived! He would never tell you to pray for something that could not happen, so if He warns us, we must take heed!

The Bible states there is going to be a great falling away. We are going to watch people we love fall away. Why? Because they stood stiff. In comparison, wheat bends over. Why? Because from the heaviness of their fruit, they bend. The fruit of their life bent them over. Why? Because when we walk in obedience to God, our life is full of fruit.

I do marriage counseling all the time, and as I start talking to couples, one of the first issues that present itself is the issue of communication or money. I begin by saying, "You know we can spend all day dealing with the leaves. Or we can get to the root. How is your relationship with the Lord?" Whenever they say their relationship is terrible, I say, "Let's fix that." When they realign themselves with the Lord, everything else falls right into line. Why? Because the fruit of an obedient relationship with the Lord is that everything in your life prospers. When you are off with God, everything suffers. But when you and Jesus are in sync, everything is blessed. Not perfect, but blessed.

My amazing father suddenly went to be with the Lord in January 2021. I had just ministered at a funeral that morning, and my brother, also a pastor, ministered at a funeral that day. That same day we got a phone call from my mom that my dad had collapsed, and we rushed to the hospital. We entered the waiting room with lifted hands and prayed. The doctor walks in and says, "What in the world is going on in this room?" I said, "What is it, doctor?"

He answered, "I have never seen a family with this catastrophe be so calm and at peace." My response was, "Oh, we believe in a Sovereign God. We believe in a God that is the owner of life and death. We believe in a God that is able to do whatever He wants, and our answer to God is always "Yes."" My father has lived an incredible life, raised two children that are preachers of the Gospel, and blessed our lives in many, many ways. And if it is time for him to get his reward for how he has lived, we will weep for him, but we will bless him." And the doctor did not know how to react. I said, "We are heartbroken, but my father's life is full of fruit. You know why? Because he always said "Yes." He always said yes to God." The following morning he died.

When you live a life that is yielded before God, surrendered, your life is full of fruit. Surrendered to what? Life *Under* His Word, not *Over* His Word. I am not here to judge God's Word. I am here to surrender to it and to yield to it. And when I yield to His Word, my life becomes full of fruit and full of the Spirit of God. But the corrupt church is going to stiffen. They will stand nice, tall, and arrogant; they will have a form of godliness because they will quote the Word, but they will be powerless. God will not be in it.

I need you to hear me; the time will come when the itchy-ear church will outnumber the Remnant. While the itchy-ear, culture, and emotionally-driven church will outnumber the Remnant, it is the Remnant that will have the power of the Holy Spirit. We, the Remnant, will have Daniel power, Shadrach, Meshach, and Abednego power, the fourth man showing up in the fire kind of power, cancer falling off of people's bodies, and the dead being raised type of power. But the Remnant will have to be prepared. Walking and remaining with the Lord will cost us everything. And

I have said to the Lord, "You are worth it, King Jesus. You are worth it. Take it all. If the cost of remaining grounded in You, walking in and surrendering to Your Word, and speaking the truth costs me everything, have at it, have at it!" Many people have stopped speaking the truth because they are afraid. We must start opening our mouths as the Church and speak the truth in love. At all costs, speak the truth. If that is going to cost us everything, He is worth it. It cost Him everything to redeem us. Now it is our turn.

And so, the challenge before us is this: Each of us has to decide – on which side of the cement we are going to stand on. Will we allow culture, our emotions, and the itchy-ear of our flesh to drive us? Or are we going to live surrendered and yield before the Lord until Jesus comes. Are we willing to hate what He hates and love what He loves, even if it costs us everything? Even if nobody wants to talk to us anymore, even if it costs us, are we willing to be of the Remnant? Do we want to be that which remains? Each person reading this has to make a decision. Who will you be? Are you going to be the tare that stiffens and manipulates the Word of God, deciding what you will obey and what you will not obey? Or are you going to be the wheat whose life is full of fruit because you are yielded under the Word of God, and submitted to the Word of God in obedience?

Today, are you willing to say *yes*? Are you willing to say, I want to be part of the Remnant. I want to be one of those that remain. If your answer is yes, I want you to pray with me!

Declaring: *"God, I am yielded to You, King Jesus. I am not going to be driven by my emotions. I am not going to be driven by culture. I surrender under your Word today. What You love, I love. What You hate, I hate. I yield, God. I am yielded, and I am surrendered. Lord, my cry is that I would be part of those that remain, the Remnant people. Father, I do not want to be the itchy-ear church. I recognize that the days are dark, and they continue to get darker, but Lord, I'm determined that as they get darker, I am going to go deeper. I am going to spend more time in your presence, God.*

I am going to surrender more and seek you more, God. I am not going to shift with culture, God. I am not going to shift with my emotions. I will not alter your Word but surrender to it, God. I yield, King Jesus, I yield. We are so grateful that You win, King Jesus.

We rejoice today, God. We feel the mantle that you have put on us. We are so privileged that you chose to trust us at this moment with this mantle. We feel the weight of that mantle. Our job is to advance your Kingdom. Father, give us the plan, give us the words and give us the anointing. Open up the windows of Heaven, God, and pour out your revival on us. Pour out Your Spirit. As we yield before You, have Your way.

In the Matchless Name of Jesus, Amen!"

A Tree Planted

We serve a faithful God who is able to do exceedingly, abundantly more than we could hope or imagine. This is the time of great faith and the time for the people of God to dwell in great faith.

The church should not look like the world. The church began to be full of compromises and afraid to offend. We were afraid to live lives that were faith-filled and lives that were filled with the presence of God. We were coasting our way through. And so God began to speak to me, "Will you take a step of faith? Can I use your life?" My answer was, "Of course, God, you can." Shortly after, I resigned from my full-time pastoral position. Let me share a little bit of my story. I am Egyptian and a New Yorker. I live in New Jersey because my ministry is there, and I have been pastoring since I was 18. I have pastored many different churches through the years. I pastored a fully-ethnic church where God allowed me the honor of being the first female ordained Egyptian in the Assemblies of God on the East Coast. That had never happened before and was unheard of. But in this season, God has raised me up to help empower the Church to stand with courage in the hour that we live in!

I had a good job, a nice salary, health insurance, everything included, and I stepped away 100% with no plan B. So I burned the plow and told God "I was in" and would do whatever He wanted. And with that, in 2020, I became a full-time revivalist.

In the course of this calling, I have seen God do great things. As I shared in the intro, I host an online prayer meeting. Listening one night was the family of a woman who was on her deathbed with Covid. Doctors had called the family three times to say their goodbyes. Each time they refused to say 'goodbye.' Instead, we prayed and stood with the family in faith. That woman is home now, delivered and set free. God is good! We have testimony after testimony of God doing work all around the world!

The enemy has also been busy. He released sickness with Covid. But what has also been released, in addition to sickness, is a spirit of fear that has gripped hearts. The pandemic was the enemy's opportunity to release fear. I was on a plane, and I had a cough. This elderly couple sitting next to me sprayed me with Lysol. They even began to spray it on my face! They literally wanted to stop the plane. Through all of this, I knew they were just terrified. They were not trying to hurt me. It was a spirit of fear. When asked if I wanted to press charges, I declined, knowing they were just terrified.

In addition to the spirit of fear, other events were occurring: riots, social justice issues, and lawlessness. A spirit of lawlessness was released where people do not understand what is right and what is wrong. We were watching it right before our eyes. The Church must learn how to respond. It cannot play a defensive game; it has to play an offensive one. We must understand who we are in this time and in this hour. God has equipped us, the people of God, to stand for Him in this hour.

Right now, God is allowing His Church to be the Church. Let me explain further; there was a church that was birthed in the book of Acts, but that is not the church that's represented today. The calling of a revivalist, and the revival that God wants to pour out, is to bring the Church back to its original condition. What the pandemic did for the Church was great! But, you may ask, *How can that be?* It shook the Church and left it with three things: preaching, praying, and worshiping. Everything else is gone. We have to understand what God is doing in this season and at this time. He is preparing us for the most significant revival ever to hit His Church, and He is preparing us for His second coming.

The verse that marks this season is found in Isaiah 5:20. "Woe to those who call evil good, and good evil; who put darkness for light, and light for darkness; who put bitter for sweet, and sweet for bitter!" That is where we are now; everything is flipped on its ear.

When you get a driver's license in New York City, there are now three choices for gender: male, female, and X. This is evil because it is completely spitting in the face of God and what He created. We need to understand that the greatest things against the Church are not attacks from the outside; we can see those. What comes against the Church very clearly is the spirit of deception. How many have seen people who you thought were solid believers post things that cause you to wonder what they were thinking? How many have seen people who you thought understood the Word of God putting out things so contrary to the Word of God?

The Bible tells us that in the last days, there will be a great falling away. So what should we do? First, we are to stay alert and not be confused or deceived. We need to understand, at this time and in this hour, how we are to live, how we are to walk, and how we are to stand.

In Jeremiah 17, the prophet Jeremiah is writing at a time when the people of Israel are becoming very confused. They are beginning to follow different teachings. They don't understand what is happening around them and are utterly confused. Jeremiah, being the prophet that he is, begins to speak the 'truth.' The Church, at this time, must have a voice and stand the way Jeremiah did. Martin Luther King questioned whether the Church was a thermometer or a thermostat. He said in the early days of the Church, "the Church was not merely a thermometer that recorded the ideas and principles of popular opinion; it was a thermostat that transformed the mores of society." There is a big difference between a thermometer and a thermostat. A thermometer indicates what the temperature is. A thermostat regulates the temperature. It is time for the Church to understand its role. We are not here to adjust to circumstances. We have done that for too long. We started fearing popular opinion and did not want to offend or hurt people. We did not want people to leave the church. And so, we adjusted and adjusted, and what left was the power of God.

We are now at a place where we need to be a thermostat, where we begin to say, *No, this is the Word of God, this is the truth of God, this is the understanding of God.* We need to speak it with clarity, and we need to speak it with understanding. And so Jeremiah begins to instruct the people of Israel. In their confusion, he tells them to allow him to help them understand how they are to think, how they are to process, and how they are to stay true to the end.

Throughout my journey, God continues to say that only two churches will remain. There will only be the corrupt church and the Remnant. Everything else is gone. Forget about Baptist, Pentecostal, etc. There are going to be Remnants sprinkled throughout all the denominations. Those who remain true are the Remnants. While both churches will use the Word, one will yield to the Word, and the other will manipulate the Word. The corrupt church will stand *over* the Word and say, "This is what it means." On the other hand, the Remnant Church will go *under* the Word and say, "God, what do you mean?" It is a very different posture, but that is the difference between the two churches. I am determined to remain part of the Remnant; I am determined to stay under the Word and say, "Lord, You speak. I am not going to tell You what You mean." I am not going to demand God's Word yield to me. I am going to yield to His Word.

And so Jeremiah does this for his people. He begins talking to them and starts with these verses, which are found in Jeremiah 17:5-9. "Thus says the Lord: Cursed is the man who trusts in man and makes flesh his strength, whose heart departs from the Lord. For he shall be like a shrub in the desert and shall not see when good comes, but shall inhabit the parched places in the wilderness, in a salt land which is not inhabited. "Blessed is the man who trusts in the Lord, and whose hope is the Lord. For he shall be like a tree planted by the waters, which spreads out its roots by the river, and will not fear when heat comes; but its leaf will be green, and will not be anxious in the year of drought, nor will cease from yielding fruit. "The heart is deceitful above all things, and desperately wicked; who can know it?"

What God is telling His people in verse 5, is that if you trust in man, in what people do and say, you are cursed. If you are looking for strength from man, you are cursed. Man has no strength for you. Man is disloyal and fails. I am not here to trust in man. Man cannot lead me. Cursed is the one who trusts in man and who finds strength in man. If I am looking for people to hold me up, I curse my own life. Jeremiah is saying *cursed is that person because that person has turned his heart away from the Lord.* Man is not meant to be trusted. No man!

When I do marriage counseling, I tell the couple, "Your commitment today is not to one another, because this man will fail you. This woman will fail you." Anyone who has been married for more than five minutes can say, *Amen.* You married a human being, and as wonderful as they are, they mess up. That is the truth. We fail each other with our best intentions. It does not have to be wicked intentions. It could be the best intention. You will fail each other. Cursed is the man who trusts in man. Your heart will depart from the Lord because that is not a man's place. That is God's place. God is for me to trust. But if you trust in man and draw strength from man, your heart is turned from God. The person who trusts in man, the Bible is clear, will be like a shrub in the desert.

You will have no moisture, life, prosperity, or blessings. You will dwell in parched places in the desert and in the salt land where no one lives. When I trust in man, everything about my life is dry. Everything about my life is empty. Nothing in my life prospers. And even if prosperity comes, I will not see it because I am trusting in man. He is telling the people of Israel, you have put your trust in the wrong place. That is why you are dry and brittle and not growing. You are not prospering because you have trusted in man. The Church is where it is right now because it has put God aside and begun to trust in other things.

We have trusted in ourselves. We have trusted in our own abilities and resources. God is in third, fourth, and fifth place. Take a look at Africa. They don't have anything but God. My first mission trip to Africa was to Tanzania, a beautiful but very dangerous area. Security instructed us not to leave the spot where we were ministering, especially the women. We were to stay in that specific spot. We were to preach, pray for people, and return to the truck immediately. So we preached, prayed, and people started getting healed throughout. A woman suddenly approached me, grabbed my hand, and began speaking to me in Swahili. Knowing I could not understand her, she went to get the translator. The woman wanted me to go with her.

We asked her where she wanted me to go, and she answered, "About five blocks down." Picture this, it is nighttime, and it is pitch black! Africa has no street lights; the only lights we had were the ones we brought. Looking five blocks down, I could see nothing. I asked, "Where am I going?" I was told, "We want you to pray for someone who is sick." They were desperate, and I felt the Lord say, "go." I turned to the translator and asked him to come with me. And when I asked security, they said, "You can go, but be careful." So I took a translator, one security guard and began to walk in complete darkness. We were then guided into this place that was a box, probably the size of a small bathroom. That was their clinic.

It had a little shower curtain for privacy. There were no tools or medicine, just a space. And there sat a beautiful African mama holding a baby. I was told the baby was dying, completely dehydrated, and suffering from malnutrition. "We can't get a drop of water into her. We have tried all the IVs. They collapse because she is too weak." They even tried putting an IV in her head and neck, but nothing worked; that was their last attempt. The veins kept collapsing. I turned to the doctor and asked, "What's next?" He said, "Nothing," and walked away. That had been their final attempt, and they gave up.

I asked, "Mama, you sent for me?" "I did." "Why?" "Pray to Jesus." she said. I asked what would happen if Jesus did not heal her baby today. "I will bury her by the morning," she answered. This baby was wrinkled like a prune from dehydration. At 18 months old, she was so wrinkled; she looked like she was 90. Yellow eyes were rolling in the back of her head. She could not keep her head up and was so weak. I then leaned forward, and I began to pray in the Name of Jesus. I began to pray with faith. I did not even finish my first sentence when, all of a sudden, she sat up. Her skin began to straighten out in front of me, and her color became this beautiful caramel color. She sat up and focused her eyes on me. By the time I finished praying, she was holding my hand and laughing, completely and totally healed. I asked mama for the baby's name, and she said, "Beatrice." I will never forget Beatrice. She grabbed my face and kissed it. I asked, "Mama, who healed her?" She said, "Jesus, Jesus."

For people in Africa, there is no plan B. That is it. Either Jesus shows up, or there is nothing. That is why He shows up. People ask me why I see so many miracles in other places. The answer is they do not have anything else. They trust only in God. So God prospers the lands for them. Miracles show up for them. But if I trust in man, I have nothing. We are famous in America for saying, "I got this, I got this." Let me tell you something, you have nothing.

I am not here to trust in myself. My strongest place is trusting in Him. One Father's Day, I was preaching and spoke directly to the men, "Men, you know we do you a disservice because we make you think that your greatest strength is how you can provide. That is not your greatest strength. Sure, it is part of your portfolio, but your greatest strength, as a man of God, is teaching your family how to depend on God."

My father passed away suddenly in 2021. When someone so dear to you passes, you begin to play out your life. When I was twelve years old, my father lost his job. We had just bought a brand new house in Staten Island, and that same week, he lost his job. As he walked up the front stairs, I could tell something was very wrong. He told us he and his whole department had been laid off. I asked, "Dad, what do we do?" He responds, "What we always do. We go to the King of Kings and the Lord of Lords." So we knelt and prayed.

That was the first time I heard a prophetic word, I was only twelve. I repeated those words to my Dad. "God said you are going to be the head and not the tail." I had never read that verse. I did not know it; I was a kid. I said, "But God said to me you are going to be the head, not the tail." By the end of the day, he had four job offers! The greatest thing we can teach our children is how to depend on God. Not to depend on man. The person that depends on man will be parched and dried.

Do you have a struggle with your finances? Who I depend on is my source, not my resource. People asked how I could just quit my job and be left with no source of income. The answer is easy; my job was never my source; it was a resource in my life. My source has always been God. I have never worked for a paycheck. I have always worked for the Lord. If a paycheck happens to come, great. That is the difference; God is my source.

Nothing in my life is dry or parched if I make God the source of my everything. He is the source of my strength, power, and prosperity. But if I make myself the source, everything is parched. Jeremiah goes further when he says, "blessed is the man who trusts in the Lord, and whose hope is in the Lord." What does trust mean? Fully relying on Him. For what? Everything. God makes it very easy. Fully rely on Him for everything: my life, my source, my breath.

Every day we look at social media and see things we find so hard to believe. We can no longer use the term *pregnant women*. Pregnant women should now be referred to as *a birthing person*. Have we all lost our minds? Some of it seems comical, and some of it is downright sad. But my confidence is in the Lord. That is the difference. I don't watch the news to watch it. I watch the news to change it. That is the authority we have as the Children of God.

I had just started the prayer meetings when the 2020 riots began. I saw a man on the news. He was homeless, and I didn't know anything else about him. I saw that all his possessions, everything he owned, were burned by rioters. He was crying on the news, saying, "I don't have anything. I only owned one bag, and now I have nothing." My heart went out to this man. So in the middle of the prayer meeting, I began to pray, "Lord, I don't know who he is, but Lord can you send believers to him to help him?" The next day, one of the people who prayed with me sent me a post. A church in Texas found the man and gave him a tent, air mattress, food, and supplies. He said, "I've never had so much in all my life." I believe that was a direct link to prayer. I believe in prayer. And so I don't watch the news to watch it. I watch the news to change it. I see the news and say, "Oh no. I have authority, and in Jesus' Name, you will not. You will not teach our children at five years old about masturbation." I refuse.

We pray, and we stand. I looked at the statistics, and human sex trafficking had increased by 900% during the pandemic. 900%. Pornography among children, 900%. And so I pray against it. "Lord, shut them down. Shut them down and have them arrested. Give our law enforcement wisdom." We are watching God: 120 delivered in Florida and 122 delivered in Missouri. We are watching it as we pray and stand as the people of God, trusting with our confidence in the Word. Our confidence is in our authority. Our confidence is in the faithfulness of God. Blessed is the man who trusts in God that when we look at all these things, we can say, *My confidence is not in this. My trust is in Your faithfulness, God. My trust is in Your Word. I believe Your Word and I will be wrecked, but I will stand right here. My confidence is in the character of Jesus Christ.* It is in His faithfulness we stand.

When my mom needed emergency surgery in 2010, they told us they were unsure of the outcome. That it was touch and go. I said, "No problem. Can I have your hands, doctors, please, before you operate on my mother?" One was Buddhist, and the other a Muslim. They did not know what to make of this. "Give me your hands." And so they did. "You are about to open up, my mother, and my confidence is not in you." I laid hands on their hands and told them, "Before you cut open my mother, you might not know Jesus, but I am going to pray that Jesus still uses your hands for His glory." And I prayed over them, and both said, "Amen." The surgery was successful, and mom was perfect. Why? My confidence does not rely on people, bank accounts or jobs. My confidence is in Jesus Christ. "Blessed is the man who trusts in God, whose confidence is in Him." My confidence is not in my ability; it is in His ability.

As mentioned earlier, I am an immigrant kid who came here at the age of four. I am a female preacher who has had many people try to shut the door in my face. But God said, "I got you." This immigrant female kid, many years later, went on to preach at the United Nations. How does that happen exactly? Because my confidence is not in me, nor is it in my ability. It is not in who could provide opportunities for me but in God. "Blessed is the man who trusts in God, whose confidence is in Him."

That is the confidence we have as the Children of God. Blessed is the man who trusts in God, whose confidence is in Him. They will be like a tree planted by the water. Planted by the water. The water is the Spirit of God. They will be planted in the river of God. They will be planted by the water, and their roots sent out to the stream. Our roots will always be attached to God. When we trust in God, our roots come right down to His Word, which is the stream of God. His Word allows our roots to grow deep into His Word, and these roots do not fear when the heat comes.

Its leaves do not wither and are always green. How many know that in the days we are living in, things are going to get worse? But what happens to those that trust in the Lord? They are not worried about the heat. Heat means trouble.

They are not worried about the trouble. Their roots are planted in the river. Their roots are in the stream of God, and they don't care about the heat. God will protect them. They are not worried about the heat because they have nourishment from the water. The heat cannot hurt them because they are attached to the stream, and their leaves are always green. That means we always prosper. Where there is famine, the Church will be taken care of. God will make a way for those who trust Him, who are planted and are not moved when everything seems upside down because the Remnant are His people.

For example, my life salary depended on traveling and preaching, but then COVID hit, and all the churches shut down. God watched over me and sent ravens to take care of me. I lacked nothing. I was blessed and prospered. I opened up a non-profit in the middle of Covid, and one of my board members said, "I have opened non-profits before, and I have never seen this type of increase. Especially not during a pandemic." Why? Because when you are trusting in God, your leaves are always green, and you are rooted. He will always make a way. He opens doors no man can open. That is the God we serve. When we are planted in Him, His Word, and His character, trusting solely in Him, we are not worried about the heat, for our leaves will always be green.

He makes a way. God said they do not have to worry about the year of drought. When all the other waters dried up, the tree planted by the river did not need to worry about the year-long drought, for there is always moisture, prosperity, and blessing. Where there is no moisture, He will make a way. There were shortages of everything during Covid. Where was everything? Take toilet paper, for example! Every house that I visit now has a wall of toilet paper. They are preparing for Armageddon! Walls of toilet paper. Why? Because they are afraid of shortages. Church, when we are planted by the river, we do not have to worry about the drought.

Child of God, trust in Him, and you will lack nothing. When my family entered this country, we were only allowed to bring $750 ($250 per person) and had to leave all our other money in Egypt. My parents had to make a living, and for that, they trusted God. My mother tells the story of her first birthday here in America. My father was an incredibly generous man. When he asked my mother what she wanted for her birthday, she said, "I want nothing," because she knew they had no money. "Tell me what you want. I'll get it for you." Again, "I don't want anything." What she really wanted was a standing hair dryer, like the kind you see in salons. However, she did not say it because my father would have given up everything to get it for her. So, that day, he prayed and said, "God, I want to bless her. God, what do I give her?"

Where we lived, every apartment had a slot for its trash. On my mother's birthday, there was a box in our slot with my mother's name. My father looked and thought, "What in the world? Who even knows our name?" He picked up the box and carried it home. He said, "Madeline, this box is for you." "What is it?" And as she opens the box, she realizes it's the hair dryer she wanted, brand new and with her name on it. Why? Because my father was not afraid of the year of drought, and we should not be afraid of the year of drought. When we trust in God, He knows our simple prayer requests and innermost desires, and He provides them because He is a good Father. We don't have to worry about what is lacking in the world. Our source is not the world. Blessed is the man who trusts in God. Blessed is the man whose confidence is in God. They will be like a tree planted by the river, and they are not afraid of the year of drought. Let there be a drought. My source is not there. My source is with the King of Kings and the Lord of Lords, who can bring a hair dryer to a woman in Brooklyn because she wanted it, not because she needed it, but because she is His daughter.

That is how God operates with His people. Scripture says further, "And never fail from bearing fruit." Not only will you have enough, but you will also bear fruit. You are going to be able to give to your neighbors. You are going to be able to give to those around you. In the year when there is drought, you are going to have enough, and not just financially. But you will have joy, peace, strength, and faith. You will be able to have such a testimony to share with those around you that they will run to you and say, *How do I do this? How do I walk in favor like this? How can you be so blessed when everything else is falling apart?* And you can then tell them that your trust is not in anything but in Jesus.

During the pandemic, what did people lose hope in? The answer is everything! The medical system failed, our jobs failed, and everything else did too. Why? Because we were never supposed to trust in those things anyway. Never. And God has brought us back, saying, *I will teach you how to walk this out properly. Plant yourself in My Word, plant yourself in My character, plant yourself in Who I am today. Get your roots down deep, and you will not have to worry about the drought. You do not have to worry about the heat, and you will never cease to bear fruit. You won't just have enough for yourself, but you will have enough for those around you.*

At the end of Jeremiah 17, we read, "The heart is deceitful above all things and desperately wicked; who can know it?" You may wonder what that verse has to do with the rest of that passage. That verse is the caveat for all the previous verses. What is stored in your heart? Your emotions. And He is saying your emotions are deceitful. They are deceitful above all things. And it is our emotions that drive us. We have a generation of people who operate 1000% by their feelings. They say, *this is what I feel,* and God is saying, *No, no, you are not supposed to operate by what you feel.* Your emotions are desperately wicked. They cannot lead you. It bothers me when people say to follow your heart. Don't follow your heart because the Bible says it is deceitful and desperately wicked. Don't follow your heart. Follow the Word! The Word often asks you to do something you don't feel in your heart, which is why God is saying your heart is desperately wicked. Do not listen to it. Do not listen to your emotions. When people say, *I have my reasons, my opinions, and this is my truth.* No, there is only One truth. There are not multiple truths, for there is only One truth. Everyone has an opinion, but that does not make it true. Does that make it true just because 9 million people liked it on your Facebook page?

It is still an opinion. There is only One truth. There will be times when I read the truth, and my emotions will say, *I don't want to do it*. How many love the verses that tell us to bless those that do you harm; do not repay evil for evil, but overcome evil with good? I might not want to repay evil for evil, but I do not necessarily want to do good. My emotions do not want to do good. My emotions will tell me everything contrary to this Word. So I cannot trust them. I must understand that if I trust in God, it will be contrary to my emotions.

Will emotions tell me to leave my job, my salary, all the ministries I ran, and my health insurance for nothing? For nothing! People tried to counsel me to ensure that this step was truly from God. But they know me well enough to know that I had heard God. Sometimes God asks us to do crazy things. But our emotions cannot lead us. Look at anything great that happened in Scripture. Go to the Red Sea and lift up your hand. Ridiculous, right? Go to the Jericho wall and sing to it. Ridiculous. Go to battle and grab a guitar. Ridiculous. Do you want meat? Great! Now go outside, and I will drop quail in your hand. Ridiculous. Your emotions will fight all these things. And the Bible warns us that our heart is desperately wicked. Desperately wicked. No one can know it. So if you are going to live trusting God, believing in God, and living and walking in God, then the way to do it is to check your emotions and know that emotions have no place here.

We are now people that enter this place of great faith. We must say, *God, we are going to believe You. We are going to trust you. Our medical systems might fail, and our supermarkets might be empty. Things might go, and our banks might close. We do not know what tomorrow holds, but we know who You are, and we trust You.* Blessed is the man who trusts in God, whose confidence is in the Lord. He will be like a tree planted by the river that will always have vegetation. He is not afraid of the heat. The leaves are always green, and they never cease to bear fruit.

No More Excuses

I will open up this chapter with a prayer.

Father, I give You praise, and I give You honor. I thank You that You are such a good and faithful God. I thank You for having a plan for every person reading this book. Father, I pray that as they read this word, You would pierce their hearts and that Your Word would be like a sword cutting through them, dividing the bone and the marrow. I pray that You would produce truth in their lives, Lord God and that that truth would propel them forward in what You have for them. I pray they will be marked and changed by the power of Your Spirit. Amen.

Before I begin, I want to introduce the term kairos moment. A kairos moment is a moment when God is speaking, and that word requires a response. It requires action. It is not delivered for information; It is a speech that requires a response. Let's break down this terminology (kairos moment) together. It is important because I feel we have a misunderstanding in the Church. Often, when we think about God speaking, people will ask, *Well, did God speak audibly?* And my response is no; as a matter of fact, God's audible speech is very rare. Does it happen? Absolutely! He shows up to Moses in a burning bush, and He speaks. He shows up to Abraham and speaks; however, those moments are rare. If God has to yell out of heaven to get our attention, then something must be very wrong. God's audible speeches are for very specific moments in time and history. The way God desires to speak to His people is described in Isaiah 43:19.

It says, "Behold, I do a new thing, Now it shall spring forth; Do you not know it? I will even make a road in the wilderness and rivers in the desert." What is the meaning behind this passage? I can hear God say, *Can you not perceive it? Can you not sense it? Do you not understand? Do you not feel what I am doing? Behold, I do a new thing. Can you not perceive it?* The Scripture says, " "My sheep know My voice and the voice of a stranger they do not know." But if you were to observe a shepherd with his sheep, there is not much dialogue between them. They are just doing life together, and the sheep know his inclinations. When the shepherd stands a certain way, they know they will be fed. When he walks in a certain direction, they know they are going for a walk. They can discern their shepherd's intent because they are doing life with him.

God, like the shepherd, is looking for people that want to do life with Him. He is looking for people who will walk with Him every day, talk with Him every day, share in the Word, and live with Him so that they can perceive when God is doing something different. They will sense it. I am not talking about some new-age Oprah-type feeling. I am talking about discerning the Holy Spirit, knowing God is doing something different. Family, if God has to yell to get our attention, there is something very wrong with our walk. The Scripture calls that being "spoon fed" or living on milk. If God has to get our attention by saying *'Hey'* every time, something is wrong. The Bible says, *you've come to a place now where you need to start eating meat and be able to discern what*

God is doing. You need to be able to feel the difference in the atmosphere when God is shifting things and changing things.

People have asked me questions like, *Did God speak to you? Did God speak clearly? Did you hear God audibly say out of heaven, to step out of pastoring and step into being a full-time revivalist?* My answer is, No, nothing like that. The way it happened was that I began to perceive a new season. I began to sense something different. I began to sense a change. I began to ask myself, "What is this? What is this God? What am I perceiving?" What I did next was the exact same thing we should all do when we perceive something: I leaned into it. Child of God, when you lean into what God has placed on your heart, you begin to pray into it. Ask God, "What am I sensing here? What are You doing?" You almost create a rhythm when you begin to lean in. You begin to lean, and you keep perceiving, leaning, and perceiving. And that is exactly what I did. I kept leaning until this word showed up, and it was clear what God was doing. It was also clear what He was saying. That is often how you will hear the Lord.

Again, I did not have an audible voice that yelled out to me from Heaven. I perceived what God was doing and leaned into it until I had clarity. God desires to speak to His people that way. He desires to give us clarity as we walk after Him. I need you to understand something about God I have learned through my years of serving Him. God has two speeds. I am convinced of this! I have no Scripture to back me up, but I am convinced. It is either *Pause* or *Run*. If you have served God long enough, you will already know that those are His speeds. Here is an example of *Pause*: "God, I don't know what You are doing. Nothing is moving. I am praying, but nothing seems to be shifting. Example of *Run*: is when you have to say, "God, wait. I can't keep up."

I've learned that He is doing so much in the *Pause; even* though you don't feel anything, He is doing so much. You are learning and growing. You simply don't realize it. He is stretching you. He is teaching you. Then in the *Run*, you apply all the things you learned in the *Pause*. That is what He does. Why? Because God is always moving us forward. Again, God is always moving us forward; 'Us' meaning His Church and 'you' as an individual. God's heart is that you never stay stagnant in one place. That is what I call yesterday's manna. God always provides fresh manna. God is always moving us forward and desires His people to move forward.

Sometimes, God might show you your past for a moment, to pick up some things or to drop some things off, but it is only for a moment. He is the God of the present, not the God of the past. He does not operate in the past. The past is the past, and then it is done and over. Today is a new day, and God is looking for people that will get in line and move with him on this new day. He is looking for his people to say, "God, I know you are speaking to me, I am in, and I want to move forward." Some may ask, *Why does God always want to move us forward?* The answer is simple: God always has more. We serve a limitless God. I repeat, we serve a limitless God! Why would you ever choose a limited life? We serve a limitless God who always wants to give us more. More of what? Everything: provision, deliverance, healing, and freedom. I can stay here all day and list everything He wants to give you. God is looking to equip His Remnant Church with all the fullness of heaven in this last hour.

If you want to understand the heart of God, it is summed up very simply: God wants His Church to walk in His fullness; that is the heart of God. I repeat, God's heart is for His Church to walk in His fullness. How do I know that? Because I know He died, he died so His Church would have His fullness. Jesus said, "I have come to give you life and life more abundant." That is His mission statement; those were His words! "I have come to give you life and life more abundant." We serve a God who wants to pour Himself out into and through us. He wants to give us more. He wants us to walk in everything He has for us. He doesn't want sickness, infirmity, bondage, or anything to hold us. He wants us to walk in His fullness. He wants to bless us; He wants to bless you. He wants to pour out over you. He wants to propel you forward into everything He has for you.

He does not want anyone to remain stuck, unable to move. The issue is not God; it is us. We are actually in the way of God's fullness; God is simply waiting for us to continue moving forward like he always wants to. God is always propelling us forward. God can speak every day, all day long, but nothing will happen unless His Word is met with action from you. You will not find anyone in Scripture who received everything God had by standing still or warming a chair. It did not happen. It only happened when they moved. A step of faith had to happen - that was the requirement.

You may ask, *Why does God need my step?* He's God; it is that simple. Along with that first step, there is something called faith, and faith is the currency of heaven. Understand this point clearly. If you want to make an exchange in heaven, it must be made through faith. If you want to make an exchange on earth, it must be made through dollars. If you want to make an exchange in heaven, it is through faith because that step you take requires faith.

Once you start speaking out of faith, you are speaking God's language. Faith is the language that God can relate with, and it is like He is saying; *There you go, now you understand me. Now you are speaking my currency.* As you begin to speak this way, you can begin to step into what God has for you. It requires a step. It requires an act of faith. The Bible says that without faith, you cannot please God. It does not matter what else you are doing. If you do not have faith, you cannot please Him. The language of God is faith. That is what He speaks. I am going to be honest with you, the only thing that will stop you from receiving all God has for you are excuses, your excuses.

Excuses will stop you from walking into everything God has for you. The title of this chapter is *No More Excuses* because we will do away with the excuses. My heart is for the Church to be the Church we see in the Book of Acts. I scream the house down when I preach because I want the people of God to walk in their fullness. I want to see the Church be "The Church." I don't want to see sickness; I don't want to see disease, and I don't want to see brokenness. I don't want to see the people of God living in lack or fear, not when we serve a God that is so abundant. The only thing that will stop you are your excuses. They might be your reasons, but every reason becomes an excuse after a while. There is an urgency in the Spirit for the Church to get ready and be the Church God needs in this hour. No more excuses!

We have plenty of reasons why we don't go to the gym. We say *it's too early, my work hours,* or whatever reason we come up with.

Ultimately, we make time for what we want to make time for. I will find time because it matters to me, and you will find time if it matters to you. At the end of the day, every reason becomes an excuse. Now, let's dissect this through Scripture and I pray you have ears to hear today and are transformed by this chapter's end. John chapter 5:1-11 is the text I want us to look at.

"After this, there was a feast of the Jews, and Jesus went up to Jerusalem. Now there is in Jerusalem by the Sheep Gate a pool, which is called in the Hebrew, Bethesda, having five porches. In these lay a great multitude of sick people, blind, lame, paralyzed, waiting for the moving of the water. For an angel went down at a certain time into the pool and stirred up the water; then whoever stepped in first, after the stirring of the water, was made well of whatever disease he had. Now a certain man was there who had an infirmity for thirty-eight years. When Jesus saw him lying there and knew that he had already been in that condition for a long time, He said to him, "Do you want to be made well?" (Another version will say, "Did you want to be made whole?") The sick man answered, "Sir, I have no man to put me into the pool when the water is stirred up but while I am coming, another steps down before me.'" Jesus said to him, "Arise, take up your bed and walk." And immediately, the man was made well, took up his bed, and walked."

We see this famous pool in Jerusalem called Bethesda, which is lined all around it with the sick, the lame, and the crippled. At a certain time in the day, the water would be troubled, and whoever went to the water first was healed. Jesus shows up on the scene, and there is this man who has been sick for thirty-eight years; thirty-eight years is a lifetime! For years he has been lying by the pool, waiting for the angel to trouble the water, and then Jesus shows up. The Bible tells us that Jesus already knew everything about the man, and He said to him, "Do you want to be well?" Or, in other versions, "Do you want to be made whole?" The man gives a soliloquy as to why he has not been healed. "Sir, I have no one to put me in the water. Before I even enter the water, someone else is there before me." The man goes on and on about his plight. Jesus ignores everything he says and tells him, "Rise up and walk." The man is immediately healed.

Let's take a little deeper look into this story. Here is a man lying thirty-eight years by the pool, thirty-eight years! For some of you reading, that is some of your lifetimes. For thirty-eight years, he came every day and sat by the pool, waiting to be healed, waiting, waiting for the angel to trouble the water. He might have wanted to be healed, but he didn't *Want* to be healed. He wanted it, but he didn't *Want* it. To *Want* is a big difference. He would already be in the water if he really wanted to be healed. If that were me, I would be swimming all day! You would find me living in the water until I was healed. I would be doing the backstroke in that pool all day! The angel was going to find me already in the water.

But the man is hanging out by the pool, which has become his normal routine. The man wakes up every morning, lays by the pool, and waits, knowing he would not be healed, and then goes home. He has zero expectations. That is his norm. For some of us, our dysfunction, brokenness, and sickness are our norm, and it is just comfortable. You may say *well, it is dysfunctional, but it is normal. It is what I know.* However, the man is at the pool hanging out, and he doesn't even recognize his Kairos moment. The King of Kings and the Lord of Lords is talking to him. Jesus is speaking to him, and Jesus asks, "Do you want to be made well?" Do you notice that he does not answer the question?

He does not say yes or no but gives a litany of excuses. Jesus ignores everything he says and heals him because He is Jesus, and He is wonderful. But can I tell you this man is no different than us. We have many excuses why we do not walk in everything God has for us. We have excuses for our fear, laziness, lack of fire, and everything else.

We have a multitude of excuses as to why. We say, *God, I don't know if I have the time. I don't know if I can do this. I don't know if I'm gifted, God. I don't know if I am talented enough, God. What is this going to cost me?* At the end of the day, all of that is white noise. When Jesus was asking this man a question, there was only one answer that would suffice. Do you want to be made well, "Yes." That's all God is looking for. But he did not have that in him. He was much more comfortable being who he was than taking the risk of stepping somewhere else. Child of God, we have a litany of excuses as to why we do not walk in what God has and we do not become the people God has called us to be.

People say to me, "Pastor, you know financially we are not doing good." I then ask, "Do you tithe?" "Well, no. We really cannot tithe because blah, blah, blah." "Okay. Then you will never walk in what God has for you." It is really simple. I have had people walk into my office so sick and riddled with cancer. And as I begin to search out their life, they are full of unforgiveness. And I will say, "Well, unforgiveness is a door for sickness. Do you want to forgive?" "No, I'm sorry, I can't." And I say, "Then you'll die." That is the truth, Family, because steps are required to walk in God's fullness. I cannot be riddled with unforgiveness and expect to walk in healing. It does not work that way. I cannot tithe and do what God has called me to do and expect to be blessed. It does not work. I cannot do things my way, and the things that make me comfortable and say, God, show up and take care of everything else. It does not work that way.

All of those are excuses. They are excuses! The bottom line is this; when Jesus asks a question, there is only one answer. YES. Jesus is asking, and the answer should always be "Yes." Do you know how many good and loving people came to me when I resigned (by faith) from my church with no income and said, "Pastor, this is all wonderful what you're doing. We are excited for you. But have you thought about health insurance? Have you thought about a mortgage? Have you thought about life? Have you thought…" And I start laughing. It has crossed my mind. Of course, it has crossed my mind; I am human. But none of those are going to deter me from saying yes. They are realities, they are truths, but I serve a bigger reality. Either God is who He says He is, or He is not. Either He is the King of Kings and the Lord of Lords, or He is not. Either He is the God who speaks and then backs up His word, or He simply is not. That is the truth of it. I believe that God will take care of everything as I obey Him. He is the God who will take care of the consequences.

Do you know how I know that? The Scripture has this one little line that we just read over. It said when Jesus approached the man, He already knew everything about him. He knew everything! Do you know what that means? He knew all of his excuses before He asked the question, and He still asked the question. Why? Because He had already solved the excuses. Jesus already had a plan for the excuses. He had a plan. Think about Moses. God tells Moses to go to Pharaoh. Moses' response was, "You know I cannot speak. You know I cannot speak." So God told Moses to take his brother. "God, I don't have anything to... " "Take your stick." "But... " God did not give him a chance to finish. Whatever excuses Moses offered, God was still going to send him. Notice how Aaron never speaks every time Moses is before Pharaoh.

Moses spoke just fine when talking to Pharaoh. It was his excuse that was crippling him, and God did not let him use it. Either you will do what God says, or you will not. It is really that simple. God is saying, "I am a God that takes care of the consequences. Child of God, your job is to step into what I have for you, and I will take care of everything else." The Remnant Church that God is rising up is a fearless Church that obeys God with no excuses. They obey whatever He says and leave the consequences to Him.

You decide that you are going to walk in God's fullness. You are going to forgive. You are going to be set free. You are going to let go of the past. You are going to walk in liberty. You are going to believe in healing. You are going to walk into ministry. You are going to walk away from sin, and you are not going to be led by your emotions. You are going to do what God is telling you. Your answer is *yes*. God takes care of everything else for you because that is God.

Either we serve a God that is that big, or we all need to go home and stop wasting our time on Sunday mornings. Either He is the Lord of Lords and the King of Kings, or He is not, and we are all playing games. I am not playing games. I know the God I serve. I know how big my God is. I know that the cattle upon a thousand hills belong to Him. I know that God is able to do exceedingly abundantly more than I could hope or imagine. And God, whatever You say, the answer is *yes*. Whatever Your question is, the answer is *Yes*.

We live under these two words we throw around a lot of times. It is called 'recklessly obedient.' It is the right term. God is looking for people that will recklessly obey him. Recklessly. To say in obedience, *Yes, God, whatever you say. I am not counting the cost; that is your job. That is your job, God. My job is my obedience. Your job is everything else, God. My job is my step. Your job is everything else.* And when you live like that, miracles show up all over the place. Because God is acknowledging that we are now speaking His language. We are speaking His language of faith; the second we speak His language, He takes over. However, two-thirds of the Church will never walk in the fullness God has for them. That is so terribly sad. It is very true because they simply will not recklessly obey the Lord. I decided long ago that I would not be one of them. We obey God because it is God that is speaking. It is Jesus speaking. So in Jesus is the completion of all things. The simple fact that it is Jesus asking, the answer becomes Yes.

Let me share a story with you. On one of my many trips to Africa, we decided to go on a safari because we wanted to see the lions. That is a big deal on safari. But lions come out at four in the morning because they hunt, and then they sleep for the rest of the day. Our tour guide, an amazing tour guide at that, told us that if we wanted to see the lions, we had to get up at 4:00 a.m. and meet him.

So we got up at four in the morning and went out (just me and one other person, everyone else slept in). Picture this, you ride in a jeep with no roof, so you can lean out and look around. And as I am looking, this HUGE African bee shows up. It is big, buzzing, and loud, and it seems to like me. The bee is all around. So I swat at it, shaking it away, but it is annoying and won't go away. It is coming right up to my ear and buzzing right in my ear. So the tour guide turned to me and said, "Pastor, whatever you do, do not kill the bee." "Okay." But the bee would not go away. It kept buzzing around me and buzzing around me, and I kept swatting at him. It landed on my hair; I knocked it out of my hair. Then finally, after 20 minutes of this, it landed right in front of me on the glass. So I look at the tour guide, whose back is to me. I then take off my flip-flop (while no one is watching) and kill the bee. Well, before my shoe left the bee, about 30 to 40 more bees came out of nowhere and surrounded the truck. So I'm thinking, *What in the world?* The driver turns to me and asks, "You killed the bee?!"

"I did! What is happening?" He says, "African bees are very loyal, and when they smell the blood of a fallen comrade, they attack the person who killed that bee." I said, " Bro, you never said any of that!" He responded with this profound statement. "I should not have had to say anything." Listen to his words, "I should not have had to say anything. All you needed to know was that I knew better than you. All you needed to know was that I knew better than you." "I am so sorry. Now save my life. Get us out of here!" He puts the car in drive, and we fly 60 miles an hour across the desert. When we get to the site, he tells the men what happened. They now have to wash the truck. I have to go take a shower, and I even put on a different perfume. When I came out, I was pointed to by every employee as the Mzungu (white person in Swahili) who killed the bee. Let me tell you, the bees never left us. They chased us all day, even after all that.

Listen to what the tour guide said. He did not need to tell me all the steps. I just needed to know that he knew better than me. That is why we recklessly obey because God knows better than us. He knows better. So when He is asking a question, if your answer is "No" or "I Don't Know", you are stating that you know better than God. And you don't know better than God. He knows better. You can struggle and search for clarity but lean into it until God gives you the confidence to say yes. The second you begin to say, "God, I don't think this...," " you have now set yourself up as God, and you are not God; you are His servant. Whatever He says, my answer is *"yes."*

Let me share another story with you. I was still pastoring in New Jersey and preparing to leave for Africa on another mission trip. A separate team simultaneously was leaving for Colombia and had collected socks for the children there. The Columbia team left, but for some reason all the children's socks were left behind. Looking at them, I thought, God, what am I supposed to do with them? And at that moment, I felt prompted to take them to Africa. Now I'm thinking, take socks to Africa?! It makes no sense to me. It sounds ridiculous; Africa is hot. No one wears socks in Africa. However, I obeyed the prompting of the Lord and took all these children's socks with me.

So, I get to Africa with a suitcase full of children's socks. The second day we were there, they told us we would visit an orphanage and that we should prepare ourselves, as this is one of the poorest orphanages in the area. These children have nothing. These are kids that were found on the streets. There is no money. There isn't anything. When we get there, I see that this is truly one of the most dilapidated orphanages I have ever been to, but the children love Jesus. The place doesn't smell great, and it doesn't look great. There is no light, and there are no light fixtures. They live by the sunlight because they don't have any lamps and the children have old clothes. Everything is just poor, and all I have is this ridiculous bag of socks.

I wanted to bring a steak. Do you understand? I wanted to bring whole outfits! I wanted to bring shoes! But instead, I am carrying this ridiculous bag of socks in a reckless act of obedience to God. We then went in and were introduced to the children. "Our friends from America are here, children; what would you like to do with them?" "We want to worship." So we worshiped for the next two and a half hours with these children. And as we were getting ready to leave, I took aside the woman in charge and asked if we could talk for a minute. "I have this bag for the kids." I said, "What?"

"This bag, I have this bag for the children." I responded. "Okay," she says, "What is it?" I whisper, "It's socks."

"I'm sorry, pastor, what did you say?" she asks. "They're socks." again, I responded. "Did you say socks?" she again asks. "Yes." I responded. Well, she starts screaming, "Jesus! Jesus! Jesus!" So now I don't know what is happening. She calls all the children. "Children, come! Come quickly, children!" All the children come running over. "Children, what did we pray for two days ago?" And the children respond, "For socks." "And look what the pastor brought us today, a bag full of socks. So that means while we were praying, the pastor was already in the air with the answer to our prayer."

And you know what I learned at that moment? I don't care how ridiculous obedience makes me feel; I will obey. I will obey because God heard the cry of a little orphan in Africa that wanted pink socks, and He sent me from America to her with pink socks. I'm good with that. Child of God, each one of you will have kairos moments. Do not miss the moment! God is rising up *"a last day people"* who live in the kairos moments. You are in one today, and do you know why? Because God is asking a question today, *Do you want everything I have for you? Do you want to be free? Do you want to be healed? Do you want to be delivered? Do you want to let go of the past? Do you want to forgive? Do you want everything I have for you?* And Child of God, I tell you right now: No other answer than "Yes" will suffice. No other answer will suffice except "Yes."

Even as you are reading this, your excuses are starting to bubble up. I need you to squash them and say; *I will not excuse myself out of the will of God. I will not excuse myself from the things God has for me. I will say Yes and let God deal with all the consequences. I will say Yes and do exactly what God is calling me to do, and everything else is His business. My Yes is my business.* Don't be one of the two-thirds that never walk in the fullness of God on this earth! Walk in all He has! Stand Remnant!

It is about the Soil

Don't worry about what is happening outside. Our God is bigger. Our God is stronger. Our God is more capable. He is not afraid of the darkness, so you should not be afraid either. If the darkness does not scare Jesus, do not let it scare you. I recognize that the enemy has brought his "A game." But God has yet to bring His "A game," and when God begins to move, no one can stop Him.

We have seen an attack on our children all over our nation. The enemy has come for the most vulnerable, and I tell you, the Church cannot stand down. If you want to see the Hand of God move with great vigor, then start coming for our children. That is a different game.

The Church needs to be front and center in that battle. We do not put children on the front line. I don't know of any army that puts children on the front line. You put children behind you. You put the men and the women first. We must stand for our children because the enemy wants to take them. And we have to tell the enemy, "not on our watch." Not while there is breath in us are we going to allow Satan to destroy our children and young people. We will stand. We will be a voice, and we will be present. We are going to battle Satan in prayer. We will battle the enemy in every way that we can.

If the enemy takes a generation, we are in trouble. We will not recognize our nation in a few years. How many don't even recognize our nation right now?! Imagine if this continues. This is not about a personal attack; this is a demonic agenda, and it is straight from the pit of hell. The controversy on gender is a challenge to God's Face because the Bible says He created them, male and female, in His image. Now our nation wants children to be created in whatever image they want. Do you know that in Michigan, they have cat litter boxes for children who identify as cats in the high school bathrooms? The Bible says they were created in the image of God, and now we are letting them be created in the image of animals. And now, all of a sudden, there are over a hundred genders. Now, more than ever, the Church cannot sit quietly. There is nothing about Christianity that is or ever has been passive.

We have to understand who we are. We say we are the salt of the earth. Salt has two purposes. Salt seasons and preserves, and we as the Church, as the salt of the earth, need to preserve the things that are righteous. We need to preserve the things that are holy, and we need to preserve the godly things. We must be present as the people of God, as the salt of the earth. We need to preserve God's Word. There are only two genders; the Word is clear: God, created them, male and female.

We need to be a people who understand our role in this hour because we are not to take a backseat and wait to see what happens. We need to learn to play an offensive game, get ahead, and be the people of God right now. King Jesus is coming, and He is coming for a bride without a spot or wrinkle. He is coming for a people who are doing their job until He returns. He is preparing His people to do great work on the earth.

In Luke 8:4, we read, "And when a great multitude had gathered, and they had come to Him from every city, He spoke by a parable: "A sower went out to sow his seed. And as he sowed, some fell by the wayside; and it was trampled down, and the birds of the air devoured it. Some fell on rock; And as soon as it sprang up, it withered away because it lacked moisture. And some fell among thorns, and the thorns sprang up with it and choked it. But others fell on good ground, sprang up, and yielded a crop a hundredfold." When He had said these things He cried, "He who has ears to hear, let him hear!" When the disciples asked Jesus what this meant, in verse 11 He told them. "Now the parable is this: The seed is the word of God. Those by the wayside are the ones who hear; then the devil comes and takes away the word out of their hearts, lest they should believe and be saved. But the ones on the rock are those who, when they hear, receive the word with joy; and these have no root, who believe for a while and in time of temptation fall away. Now the ones that fall among thorns are those who, when they have heard, go out and are choked with cares, riches, and pleasures of life, and bring no fruit to maturity. But the ones that fell on the good ground are those who, having heard the word with a noble and good heart, keep it and bear fruit with patience."

While this is a familiar passage of Scripture, I want us to look at it more deeply. First, realize that the seed never changed. The seed is the seed. It is the same seed. The problem is never the seed; the problem is always the soil. Jesus talked about four different kinds of soil. Before we look into the four kinds of soil Jesus spoke about, you need to understand that the corrupt church, the itchy-ear church, will also use the Bible to its advantage. But they are going to stand over it. They will make the Bible say what they want it to say. That is why we have cults, and all kinds of religions that use the Bible. They just misuse it. The Remnant people will live under it, submit, surrender and yield. How you receive the Word of God, your posture before the Word of God, determines how the Word of God moves in your life. Your posture is the most important key to receiving the Word of God.

The first kind of soil that Jesus spoke about was the one the enemy comes and immediately steals from. How often does God speak a word to you in church, and before you leave the door, it's gone? The enemy came and stole it. He took it. The enemy is strategic and disguises his weapons. He uses familiar people to steal words. You get a word in church, but by the time you get home, you and your spouse are fighting so badly that you have forgotten what happened in church. It is not your spouse's fault, and it is not your fault. You just did not recognize the enemy and his tactics. Remember, he comes to steal that word, and if you are a wise believer, you must learn to guard God's Word.

On one of my mission trips to Africa, I went on a safari and saw a kill (yes, I love safaris). Everyone wants to see a kill on a safari. I don't know why, but they do. We saw two female lions take down a zebra. My team was almost jumping out of the truck with excitement. Fearful for their safety, I told them they needed to get back into the truck. After all, we weren't at Six Flags Great Adventure! They make you sign a waiver on a safari stating that they are not responsible for your safety. And as we were watching the two lions take down the zebra and eat their prey, suddenly, both lions jumped up and looked in one direction. We had no idea why they jumped up. As we looked around, we noticed there was a little hyena. They could sense him and just watched him. While one lion ate, the other watched, and they took turns eating. When they had enough to eat, they let out this little roar, and the hyena ran away.

The Lord spoke to me at that moment. He told me that His Church does not guard His Word the way the lions guarded their prey. His Church needs to guard it because a hyena is always looking to take it. God plants a Word, and a hyena is always looking to take it out of your spirit. God gives you something, and you, Child of God, need to learn that your soil is good. The Word will flourish in you, and you must keep that Word and not let Satan have it. I have walked away from discussions because I knew the Word God gave me was not being received the way He meant. I have had to walk away because I need to guard His Word. You get a Word about healing, and by the time you get outside, you get a phone call from the doctor that your test results were not good. That is the enemy trying to steal the Word you just received. The most precious thing we have is His Word.

The Word is the most precious thing that you own. It needs to be your bread; it needs to be your food; it needs to be your defense. The Bible is not a history book; sometimes we treat it like that. It is not a history book; it is a blueprint. If you are building a house and your contractor comes to you and tells you that he will figure it out as he goes along, maybe get the dimensions later, you would be looking for a new contractor. When the right builder walks in, he opens up the blueprints and says, *here is the plan.* That is the Word of God. It is our blueprint as believers. We do not have anything more precious than His Word, nothing. We need to learn to guard that Word and hold it deep within because an enemy wants to steal it.

John 10:10 tells us the enemy comes to steal, and to kill, and to destroy. But Jesus tells us that He has come so that we may have life and life more abundantly. Anything that comes into your life that steals, kills, or destroys comes from one place. The enemy comes to steal, kill and destroy the work of God in your life. He tries to steal the Word that God is trying to give you. The Word of God is a seed that, if planted properly, will produce more fruit in your life than you could ever imagine. The Word works. Hear me, the Word works.

The Word of God, the seed, is never the issue; it is always the soil. We have the soil that receives the Word with joy, but then troubles come, and we give up. Do you know how many believers give up right before their victory? There may be as many as two-thirds of the Church who will never walk in the fullness God has for them because they give up.

I attended Zion Bible College and the college president then was Rev. Ben Crandall. He had one sermon he preached constantly, and it was never to give up. He would finish every sentence with, "Never give up, never give up. You have no idea when your blessing is about to come. You have no idea when God will turn everything around for you." Our job as the Church is to be tenacious and grab hold of the Word of God like our life depends on it. We need to do that because our life does depend on it. That is not a figure of speech. Our lives literally depend on God's Word, and we need to grab it and not let the pressures and the cares of life rip it out of us. Never give up! I recognize that some of you have been waiting for years on a Word that God gave you. I understand, but you need to wait some more. Either He is who He says He is, or He is not. Either this Word is true, or it is not. It is one or the other. You have to decide.

In 2016, I was preaching in a church in Africa. The temperature that day was 120 degrees Fahrenheit. The church was a brick building with a steel roof, no air conditioning, no fan, and we had a four-hour service. If you have ever been to an African service, they have "church." We are lazy in America. They really have church. During that service, one shy girl on my team tried to hide during worship. The Africans came and scooped her up and made her dance with them; that's what I mean when I say they have church. They are there because they have walked two hours to get there. We have an American Christianity; we don't understand that. We get annoyed if the drive to church takes more than 40 minutes. The American church is lazy in comparison to the rest of the churches around the world. We are comfortable. Many walk two hours to church in suits because they are going to worship Jesus.

And they worship. Their jackets come off, and they are there for church. That day, when the service ended, my throat didn't feel right. I started coughing. I sounded like a man. My voice was so raspy and I could not stop coughing. Since we were in Kampala, which was not a very clean area, I thought some dust had probably gotten into my lungs. However, it did not go away, and I was still coughing when I returned to the States. I went to the doctor thinking I had bronchitis. The doctor gave me some antibiotics, but I was still struggling. He then gave me three more medications.

Months in, and nothing was working; I was struggling to breathe. I could not catch my breath. I would walk up a flight of stairs and have to stop. I could not catch my breath. After visiting a pulmonologist, I was told that my lungs were inflamed. He did not know why, so they began to do a multitude of tests. If you have ever had any breathing tests, they are exhausting. You can't breathe, but they want you to breathe into a bag. All the while, I am getting worse. I had no energy because I could not breathe. I couldn't even wash dishes. But I am a fighter. I never stopped going to work. I never stopped pushing, but I was exhausted. I was going to bed at six in the evening. I could not keep my eyes open. I would take breaks while driving. I did not know what was happening to me. I went to different doctors. They, too, did not know what was happening to me. They sent all my medical records to Columbia and Cornell and still could not diagnose me. They were afraid I would die because my lungs were getting worse every day. My hands were turning blue. My lips were turning blue. My oxygen levels read 87 at times by just walking around.

Praying the whole time, I asked the Lord what the next tool was. I had already used all the ones I knew. I asked, *Is there another tool You want me to use?* The Lord told me He wanted me to begin to read Psalm 91 out loud every day. The same way I was to take my medication, I was to read Psalm 91. I began reading the psalm out loud. Do you know what happened? I got worse; I got significantly worse. I had pneumonia three times in one year because my lungs were so damaged. But I kept reading Psalm 91. There was one particular time I was reading, and I got so winded reading the Word that I felt like I was going to pass out. I remember saying to the enemy, "Satan, I want you to hear me. I might pass out, but I will get up and finish reading. So you can decide how this plays out, but I will do what I was told to do." The Word has power, but I did not see the power right away.

Nine months in, I am still reading the Word every day and still getting worse every day. Then one night, I came home from work and was the sickest I had ever been in my life. My hands were bright blue. I could not breathe. As I was sitting on the edge of my bed, the Lord said, "Go to sleep." So I put my head down and began to hear Psalm 91 read over me. The Spirit of God was reading it over me. I heard prayers. I asked the Lord who this was. He said, "This is the corporate body that has been praying for you all this time. I have held all their prayers because they have no expiration date. And in one moment, I am going to answer them." I closed my eyes that night. When I woke up the following morning, I jumped up because I had overslept and knew I was late to work. So I ran to the bathroom. Suddenly, I realized that I was running. I was running! I started moving around. I could breathe. Catch that; I could breathe, the Lord healed me as I slept.

I called the doctor for an appointment right away. He wanted to know why I needed to see him so quickly. I told him I needed another x-ray of my lungs. After the x-ray, he could only say, "Where did you get new lungs from? These are brand-new lungs. On the x-ray from two weeks ago, your lungs were gray. On today's x-ray, they are white." Hallelujah! He wrote on my chart all that I told him from the beginning, and then he wrote 'miraculous.' That is what it says on my chart. Miraculous. The Word works.

The Word works, but what if I had given up? What if I said after one month, *it is not working. I am worse. I am worse, God, and your Word does not work.* What if I thought I was sitting here quoting the psalm each day like it is magic? I would not be here right now! You cannot give up when you are standing; you cannot. Brothers and sisters, listen to me; you cannot give up on your children. You cannot give up on your marriage. The Word works. You cannot give up on your health. You cannot give up on anything. The Word works. Do not allow it to be taken from you. The Word works.

You have to learn to stand. The Bible tells us that having done all, to stand. Stand. That is not a misprint. He knew we would want to give up. So He said it twice. He wants His children, after having done all, to stand, to continue to stand until it happens. That is the answer. How many years? Until it happens. If you remember Joseph, in the Old Testament, he had a dream of his family bowing down to him. It took 18 years for the dream to be fulfilled, even though everything that happened in Joseph's life was contrary to the dream. Joseph had to hold on and hold on and honor God and do the right thing when all the wrong things were being done to him. Joseph is a hero of the faith. Everything that could go wrong did go wrong. But he held onto God's Word, and 18 years later, he saw it come to pass with his own eyes. The Word works. God keeps His promises. He is just looking for a people who will grab hold of His promises and not move. A people with faith and the trust to say, my God is exactly who He says He is.

The enemy is not trying to convince us that God does not exist. CS Lewis once said. When his wife struggled with cancer, he said he was not in danger of thinking God did not exist. He had seen too much. He knew God existed, but he was in danger of thinking that God was less than who He said He was. That is the enemy's tool. You will never pray if he can get you to think that God is less than who He says He is. You will never have faith. You will never have trust. You will never accelerate. You will just live a nice little Christian life and make it to heaven. Please don't do that. Please don't settle for average. Decide today that God is exactly who He says He is. He is a faithful God. He is true to His Word. He is almighty. He is the King of Kings and the Lord of Lords. He is the Alpha and the Omega. And He is our soon returning King. Do not give up, Children of God. The Remnant people are to grab hold of God's Word and not let it go.

As we see further in Luke 8:7, "And some fell among thorns, and the thorns sprang up with it and choked it." The Word is here to make you holy, but we want the Word to make us feel good. There are times the Word is going to bless you. It is going to encourage you. And then there are times the Word is going to convict you. If you feel comfortable in church every week, something is very wrong. You should sit on the edge of your seat, wondering how the pastor or preacher knows that about you. The Word, the Lord, your pastors, they all love you. We love you. True love is telling the truth. We tell the truth. If I didn't love you, I would lie to you. *Oh, whatever you feel is fine.* No. Whatever you feel is not fine. Whatever you think is not fine. You are to be transformed by the Word of God. That means your thoughts, feelings, and emotions are subject to the Word of God. It will not allow you to hate; it will teach you better. It will not allow you to hold onto unforgiveness; it will teach you better.

One day a woman walked into my office. She was riddled with cancer and asked me to pray for her healing. When I told her I could not, she wanted to know why. I responded, "You are full of unforgiveness towards your husband. You've made a roadblock.

I cannot get through that. You have to forgive first. The Bible is clear. He will not heal in that instance. It is a roadblock." She responded that she would rather die than forgive. She refused to forgive. She allowed the Word to be taken from her because she would not yield to it. She allowed it to be taken. The thorn took the Word from her, and the thorn can take the Word from any one of us if we are not careful. Don't think you are above it because that simply is not true. It is all about yielding to the Word when God begins to poke at something in your life. If He says, *check your attitude*, then check your attitude. If He says *respect*, then respect. If He says, *humble yourself*, then humble yourself. If He says *apologize*, you apologize. Get your house in order. In love, I tell you to get your house in order today. Do the work of sanctifying your life. Let the Word prick you. It is okay. It is love.

I went to India in 2011. While I was there, I bought a saree. Remember, I'm Egyptian, but I bought a saree anyway! I decided that I was going to wear the saree to preach upon my return from India. I even watched a YouTube video for instructions on how to wear it so I could put it on the best I could. That Sunday, upon my return, I was scheduled to preach during both services. After I finished preaching the first service, three beautiful Indian women came up to me and told me to come with them. They took me to the restroom because they said I looked like a "mess." They wrapped my saree correctly, and only then would they let me return to preach the second service. Do you know what I call that? I call that love. They were not going to leave me in my "mess." They loved me enough to say they had to help me.

Love does not leave you in your mess. Love calls you out. Love tells you what the Word says. Grace alone without truth is a mistake.

That is what has happened in America. We have accepted this grace gospel with no truth. They have to go together. Grace and truth must go together. Grace says everything is fine; you are okay on your journey, even if it is not. Yes, come as you are. Open the doors wide and come as you are, but you cannot stay as you are. You need to be changing every day. Come as you are but change every day. You have to have both. I grace you, and I love you. I am here, walking with you, but I will tell you the truth. Live right; live holy. The Bible tells us about living a life without reproach; that means no one can look at your life and convict you. Your life is integral. That is what the Word does; it sanctifies you. The people that lose the Word because of the thorns do not want that. They want to walk with God to a certain level, but they never mature because of what the Word requires of them. Take control of your life. I don't love everything the Word says; none of us do. I love the Word but do not want to love my enemies. Is there anyone who wants to love their enemies? Is there anyone who wants to do good to those who persecute them? Either I will mature and produce a hundredfold in my life, or I will not. It is that simple.

We have to decide and let the whole Word become a tool to make us like Jesus. Jesus did not rescue us to make us the best version of ourselves. That is worldly terminology. *Be the best you, you can be.* It is a deceptive lie. Be the best you. I hear Christians saying this all the time. I do not want to be the best me. On my best day, the best me is rotten to the core. The Bible says our righteousness is filthy rags before God. He did not save me to make me the best version of myself or make you the best you. He saved us to make us like Him.

We have been saved to be made like Jesus. It is not about making you a good person or a kind person. It is about making you like

Jesus. The Word transforms us, and the corruptor does not want you to be like Jesus. However, we, the Remnant people, want others to look at us and see Jesus. We want to reflect Him. We want to live like Him. We want to pray like Him. We want to walk like Him. We want to be like Jesus; that is the desire of the Remnant people. The corrupt church thinks: I am happy. I am living my life. I am not hurting anyone, but the Remnant people understand that getting our life in order with the Word of God is necessary. It is about submitting to the Word of God. It is about surrendering my choices, my feelings, and even my dreams to what He says and letting the Holy Spirit do surgery in my life to clean me up. We, on our own, are all hot messes.

God is looking for a people who will not allow the thorns to rob the Word from them because the Bible says they will never come to maturity. They are filled with immaturity because they will not yield to the Word of God. When they are faced with something that God requires, they back off. They would rather have their pleasure. They would rather have their choices. They feel, *what's the big deal?* It is a big deal. It is a big deal because it is robbing you of being a mature believer.

The Bible then says, there is a seed that falls on good soil. And they take deep roots, they receive the Word, and the Word produces a hundredfold in their life. Have you ever seen a watermelon seed? It is not that big. Have you ever seen a watermelon? That is called a hundredfold! The Word of God comes into your heart. It is 'rhema' meaning God's word spoken to you, and it produces fruit in your life if you allow it to. If you receive the Word with joy and gladness and allow it to grow roots in your heart, it will produce a hundredfold.

The Scripture continues, "... and bear fruit with patience." Patience. It is a word we all hate. Patience because sometimes that hundredfold takes more than a minute. A woman in my former church had prayed for 20 years for her husband to be saved. He was a good man but just did not serve the Lord. She would pray. She would fast. We were scheduling a Royal Ranger campout. Royal Rangers is a program for boys that I ran. The campout was a father-and-son event. This woman's son had never attended because his father would never go. One day I received a phone call from his dad. He knew the deadline for sign-ups for the campout had passed. He was hoping that I would not let him attend. He knew me well enough to know that I held to the deadline dates. However, I heard in his voice that he was trying to get out of this event. He told me that his son really wanted to go and that he wanted to make his son happy. But if I couldn't register them, it was not a problem. I told him to bring in the registration that day. He could not believe that I was allowing him to register. "But the deadline was last week," he said. "I know when the deadline was. It was my deadline. Come today. I'll wait for you." "I get out of work really late," he said. My response was, "I'll wait."

He knew I was not going to let him get out of it. He came with the forms and told me he really did not want to go. I told him it would make his son really happy and just to go and have a great time. While he and his son were at the campout, his wife took to fasting and prayer. Remember, she had been praying for 20 years. When he came back, he could not stop crying. I asked him what happened. Talking about our Royal Ranger Commanders, he said, "These men, they just loved me. They didn't even know me, but they loved me. They even gave me a nickname." He told me some crazy name that they made up for him. When I asked him what the name meant, he said, "I don't know. But I like it. They just loved me. Four of them surrounded me and started to pray for me. And I gave my life to Jesus."

This couple is older now, but if you watch them, you would think they were teenagers. They are so loving and so prayerful together. They live life as if those 20 years never happened. She told me that the verse that says He restores what the earthworm has eaten is now restored in her life. I have seen it with my own eyes. She has her youth and strength, and they live daily for the Kingdom. That is a hundredfold. We wait, and we take the Word, and with patience, we plant it. We water it. We nurture it. We guard it. We let it grow. We yield to it. We do whatever the Word says. Your agreement is not necessary. It is your obedience God seeks. There is a difference. I am not saying I have to understand or agree, but I do have to obey. I obey because my Father said so. When we yield to the Word, give ourselves to the Word, and allow the Word to come up in us with patience, we reap a hundredfold.

My prayer for you is that you would allow the Word to go deep and not fall into any traps but that you would mature in it. And you would go deeper into the Word and hold it with all your heart. Never give up, and know that your God is exactly who He says He is.

Are you ready to let the Word produce fruit in your life a hundredfold? Are you ready to grab the Word of God and make it your blueprint? The Word is your most precious thing; allow it to dig deep into your spirit. Yield to it entirely and wait patiently as the Word produces a hundredfold in your life.

The Word Works!

GIVE US BOLDNESS

I gave my life to Jesus at the International Christian Center in Brooklyn, New York, at the age of four. I was raised in a Christian home, but my personal walk started the day I gave my life to Him. I fell in love with Jesus that day. So when people say *children don't really understand what they are doing*, I say, "yes," *they do*. I am an example of that. Don't ever preach a junior Holy Spirit to children. They don't get a junior Holy Spirit; they get the whole deal. At the age of nine, I received the call to the ministry. At eleven, I was baptized in the Holy Spirit, and saw my first miracle. So by the age of twelve, I was wrecked by the Gospel of Jesus Christ. I don't know a small God, and I don't know a powerless God.

Growing up in church, I watched men and women of God preach, dripping from the oil of God. I would watch them open the altars and see people experience the power of God. That is what I know. I was born in the fire of the Holy Spirit. I have tasted what Church is supposed to look like. Some people go to restaurants and order a dish they have never tasted before and think that is how it is supposed to taste. But if you have been to that restaurant before, you know when they change the cook. You know when that dish is different. Why? Because you know how it is supposed to taste.

That is how I knew the Church of America had changed the gospel. Filling the buildings became more important than making disciples. Sin became acceptable and referred to as bad choices Sin is sin, no matter how you look at it, and should be addressed. We stopped holding people accountable for their life. We started using grace as a tool to let people keep sinning instead of as a gift from heaven that should convict us to live righteously. When the power of God leaves, people end up walking out of the church the same way they walked in. To me, that became unacceptable and I could not stay still.

That is when God challenged me to leave everything and step out in faith. He called me to bring revival to His Church. But I laugh because, fast forward three months from making that decision, the world shut down. Covid hit, and God strategically placed the Church right in the pocket of anticipating the greatest move of God that the Earth has ever seen. He is setting the Church up for a revival. Does that sound divine to you?

Oftentimes, I hear people say that we live in unprecedented times. Well, it is true. We do. But the Church needs to learn to look a little deeper. Unprecedented times is a worldly term. For the Remnant Church, we need to say something different. These are prophetic times. On New Year's Eve of 2020, I believe every Pastor preached the same message, 20/20 Vision in 2020. That was the title of every message I heard at the beginning of that year, and by February, everyone was blind. It was like a sandstorm, and no one could see anything. Don't misunderstand me, it is about having 20/20 vision, but it is a different vision. We must learn to look with the eyes of the Spirit, and the eyes of the Spirit are quite clear. God is doing a new thing on the Earth, and the Church needs to get the house in order. The house is the Church, and the house is our body!

God is doing that work. This is not the first time the Church has encountered the terminology of prophetic times. Throughout the course of history, there have been prophetic times when the Church needed to respond in a certain way. One of the first times was right after the Church was established. The Church was established when Jesus resurrected from the dead, and believers were baptized in the Holy Spirit. A few days later, in Acts Chapter 3, Peter and John go to pray. They come up to the gate named Beautiful. They see a lame man there who has been lying there for decades as a beggar. The man raises his hand and asks for money. Scripture tells us in Acts 3:6 that Peter turned to him, saying, "Silver and gold I do not have, but what I do have I give you: In the name of Jesus of Nazareth, rise up and walk."

Peter does not give the man a chance to answer. He grabs his hand and lifts him up. The Bible says that his feet and ankle bones immediately received strength, and he started leaping and walking. He is running around the temple, dancing, and singing and praising God. That is pretty amazing. The Pharisees and the Sadducees are beside themselves because they thought they killed their Jesus problem. They did not recognize that they created a whole bunch of other problems. There were 120 that were first baptized in the Holy Spirit. And then, there were 3,000 that were added to the Church when Peter preached his first sermon. That is every Pastor's dream; 3,000 people get saved in one sermon! Now they have 3,120 Jesus problems walking around, so they start to put them in jail. They are trying to figure out what to do about their new Jesus problems because, now, they are taking over the streets and the power of God is in them; they are anointed. These new believers are filled with passion and fire and with the anointing of the Holy Spirit.

They try to contain their Jesus problem by threatening Peter and John. But the Bible says that Peter and John began to speak and the Pharisees and Sadducees were bewildered. These are ignorant men. They are fishermen. They are uneducated. But they sound like and resemble Jesus. They could not identify the anointing. When you walk closely with Jesus, you look like Him and sound like Him. They realized that Peter and John had been with Jesus and so they tried to stop them. They threatened them, telling them they could go but could not speak to anyone in the Name of Jesus again. Peter answered "...there is no other name but the Name of Jesus" and that he must preach in the Name of Jesus. The Pharisees and Sadducees had no other alternative but to let them go because they knew the people had witnessed what happened to the lame man. Unable to do anything to them, they threatened and released them again.

The Church, at this point, comes to a prophetic moment because they must decide what to do with the threats. They have to decide, as a church, what they will do. In Acts 4:23-31, we find their response. "And being let go, they went to their own companions and reported all that the chief priests and elders had said to them. So when they heard that, they raised their voice to God in one accord and said, "Lord, you *are* God, who made heaven and earth and the sea, and all that is in them, who by the mouth of your servant David have said: 'why did the nations rage, and the people plot vain things? The kings of the earth took their stand, and the rulers were gathered together against the Lord and against His Christ.' "For truly against Your holy Servant Jesus, whom You anointed, both Herod and Pontius Pilate, with the Gentiles and the people of Israel, were gathered together to do whatever Your hand and Your purpose determined before to be done. Now, Lord, look on their threats, and grant to Your servants that with all boldness they may speak Your word, by stretching out Your hand to heal, and that signs and wonders may be done through the name of Your holy servant Jesus." And when they had prayed, the place where they were assembled together was shaken; and they were all filled with the Holy Spirit, and they spoke the word of God with boldness."

So they pray. They gather together, and they pray. And they do not pray for the threats to go away. Again, they do not pray for the threats to go away. They do not pray for an easy way out. No. They pray for boldness to preach the gospel. That is their response to the threats. They pray for boldness to do the work of the ministry. Why? Because these men were filled with the anointing of the Holy Spirit. These men had walked with Jesus. They knew Jesus and were now baptized in the Holy Spirit. They were now commissioned by Jesus to do the work of the gospel. Going back was not an option.

Jesus was too real to them. They were compelled by the mandate of Jesus to preach the gospel. Jesus gave them one instruction, *Go preach the gospel and make disciples.* They were not going to back down from that; they could not back down from that. They do not even allude to it, but they recognize that they need something. And Church, we are in the same place. It is darker than it has ever been. Do you feel it? Do you see it? It is getting darker every day. The assault on the younger generation is unreal. Satan is coming for our children and our youth with both hands. And we have to say, *not on our watch.* No way. But we need the same thing that the disciples needed. The Church of Jesus Christ right now is walking with a walker. It is limping. But there is going to come a day when the Church is going to run. God is shaking His Church. He is awakening His Church.

These disciples prayed. There are three things I take away from their prayer. They wanted courage. They wanted boldness, and they wanted the move and the power of the Holy Spirit. Courage. Courage has everything to do with the condition of the heart; it has everything to do with my inner braveness to stand. Courage is not the absence of fear. Instead, it is sometimes moving in fear. Do you know what happens when you start moving when you are afraid? The fear falls off. You just keep going. No soldier has gone into battle feeling 'I got this.' But they know they have to go. You know why? They have an allegiance to something. You cannot have courage as a Child of God if you do not have a deep intimate relationship with Jesus. Without a deep intimate relationship with Jesus, you do not know to whom your alliance is. But if I have a deep inner relationship with Jesus that is consistent, growing, intimate, and passionate, the byproduct of that is courage. I know Who I stand for, and I do not become afraid because My God is bigger than yours. It is really simple. I know Him.

David is a perfect example of this. David is a teenage boy that shows up on a battlefield. All the trained soldiers are terrified of Goliath, who comes out daily and taunts them. David comes out as a young man. He listens to Goliath. He looks around at the soldiers and does not understand their fear. David's first question to them is, "What is the reward for the one who kills him?" Meanwhile, all the other soldiers are terrified. Why did David have courage? Because of David's relationship with the Lord. He knew that the God he serves is bigger than this 12-foot giant. That relationship with the Lord did not come on the mountain, it came in the valley, it came during worship, it came in his prayer time, and it came when he was alone with God. And it manifested when he needed it. But anything will scare you if you are not in the valley with God, not in the prayer room with God, not worshiping God, or not sitting with Him. There are plenty of giants, and anything will make you run.

But when you are sitting with Jesus, in His presence, worshiping, walking with Him, talking with Him, and getting to know Him, you are prepared. Then, when this giant comes up, you are ready and prepared. *My God is bigger than you. My God is mightier than you. There is no mountain before my God.* The byproduct of your relationship with the Lord is courage. We are in a place where the Church better get some courage. It is getting darker every day. We are living the verse in Isaiah that says, "There will come a time where they will call good evil and evil good, bitter sweet and sweet bitter." We are there. We are there. Darkness has risen its head; lawlessness has risen its head. And this spirit of lawlessness is different from other spirits.

This spirit of lawlessness does not just stand opposed to God; it is now coming at the things of God. People are walking in the streets cursing Jesus. They are burning Bibles in America. I am not talking about the Middle East. I am talking about right here in America. Disgusting things are being written on church buildings. Why? Because there is an anti-Christ spirit that has risen its head, and the Church better get some courage. We better get intimate with God. Learn this; the darker it gets, the deeper

74

you go. You get deeper into the things of God, you get deeper into the Word, and you get deeper into prayer. Yes, the darker it gets, the deeper you go.

The second thing the early church asked for was the boldness to speak. To speak. Courage is about the heart, and boldness is about the voice. The Church needs to find its voice. The Church needs to speak it out. I love Charles Spurgeon, who once said, "What has cured me of the fear of man is the fear of God." The Church needs to cease being afraid of offending man and start worrying about offending God. We need to speak the truth. Why? Because we love people. If you truly love someone, you tell them the truth, and we have to tell this world *you are lost. You need Jesus.* We are compelled the same way the disciples were. We are compelled to tell people about Jesus, and we are compelled to tell people they are lost. Child of God, you have a voice, and you need to use that voice for the Kingdom. You need to declare the Word in every circumstance that you have. You need boldness. You need boldness to speak, to open your mouth and speak. Speak to people and speak to the enemy.

Yes, speak to the enemy. Speak power over your life, speak the Word of God, speak life over your children and our nation, lift up your nation in prayer, and rebuke the enemy. I rebuke the spirit of lawlessness every day. Every day. Pray for those that are on the front lines. Pray for your police officers. Pray for the things going on in our nation. Take authority as a Child of God. Use your voice, Child of God.

The final thing they prayed for was for God to stretch out His hands, heal the sick, and perform miracles. Why? Because it is impossible to deny a Living God when you see a miracle in front of your eyes. It is impossible. The Apostle Paul told the people that he did not come to them with the Gospel of the eloquence of words but came to them with the demonstration and the power of the Holy Spirit. We are a Church that is supposed to be a Church of power. The miraculous should be happening in the Church of Jesus Christ regularly. It should not be the memories of the miracles of twenty years ago. No, no, no. It should be about what is happening today!

There should be a testimony every week, every day. There is power in the Name of Jesus. There is power in the anointing, and the Spirit of God and the Church needs to move in power. We need the power of the Holy Spirit. We need signs and wonders restored to the Church of Jesus Christ. We are beginning to see increments of it, but we need more. Courage, boldness, and power work together. When you are courageous, you can stand. When you can speak, you will believe, and you will step forward to do the work of the miraculous.

I have been fortunate to have traveled to many countries. I have been to India, many parts of Africa, and Mexico preaching the gospel. It has been an incredible, incredible journey. One of my favorite places to go is Mexico because I have great missionary friends whom I have worked with for a very long time. On one particular mission trip, I was running a Vacation Bible School. When I pastored in my former church, I used to run a Vacation Bible School every year, so, naturally, wherever I go, I bring Vacation Bible School. I love doing children's ministry. On this visit, our Vacation Bible School was in this extremely poor area called El Colli. The children in this neighborhood knew we were coming, so they put on their best clothes. Their clothes are ripped and dirty, but that is their Sunday best, and it was all they had.

For example, there was a little boy whose ear had been eaten by bed bugs, and a piece was missing. There's a need in every way you could imagine. The children came starving. We learned very quickly that the mamas did not have enough money to feed their children properly, so they fed the girls on one day and then fed the boys on the other. Each day, the kids were hungry, but we found that they hid their food to feed their siblings. As a result, and as a native Egyptian, I want to give them snacks every time they attend our Vacation Bible School. I want to give them an Egyptian snack. If you are not familiar with this term, it means that it is overflowing! If you come to an Egyptian home, as a matter of fact, if you go to my mother's home, she will stand over you when your plate is half-full; she will refill it and then wait to refill it again. That is just how it is done!

On the first day of VBS, the missionary told me we would probably have about 200 children on the first day of VBS. She said they never really have more than 200 in attendance, so we were told to prepare snacks for that number. I told her I would plan for 250. On the first day, we had 250 children. So now, the next day, we prepared 270 snacks. By the third day, the missionary told me to plan for 300. On day three, sure enough, we had 300 children in attendance and just enough snacks. Nothing remained. In preparing for day four, we decide on snacks for 350. A woman was helping us who was Buddhist and lived in the neighborhood. She liked our charitable work and wanted to be a part of it. We were happy to have her help and hoped she would hear the gospel.

On the fourth day, she comes running to me and tells me we have a really big problem. She counted the children, and we did not have enough snacks. She says, "You have 350 snacks but over 400 children." "Are you sure?" I asked. She assured me, "Yes, I have counted seven times." So I ran, counted again, and stopped counting at 400 because it didn't matter; it could have been 1000 at that point. I did not have enough. There was no store to go to; there was nothing we could do. Nothing. I thought to myself, alright, *it is time for the miraculous God. We need you to show up.* So I grabbed my team, and we started praying over the snacks.

The woman walks over to me as I am praying. Remember, she is not a believer. She taps me on the shoulder and asks what I am doing. I said, "Well, praying over the snacks." And she said, "Why?" I told her the story in Scripture about the fishes and loaves. "Wait a minute, wait a minute. You think God is going to give you more snacks?" And I said, "I actually do." "Well, you are just ridiculous then," she countered. And she walked away to report me to the missionary. When she told the missionary, the missionary responded, "That's a great idea." She ran over and joined us. So now we were all praying for the snacks. So we finished praying and had all the children sit, and we gave each worker a box with snacks in it so they could hand them out.

I turned to the woman and asked if she wanted to help us distribute the snacks. "Fine," she said, but she was clearly mad at me now. I give her a box, and we start giving out the snacks. Do you remember how many snacks I had? I had 350. So we started giving out the snacks, and we hit 320, 330, 340, 350…360, 370, 380, 390, 400, 410, 420, and one box was left over; one full box was left over!

And you know who was holding that box? The Buddhist woman was holding that box, shaking, with tears on her face. I said, "You okay?" She quietly asked, "What just happened?" I said, "You tell me what happened." "They kept putting their hands in, but it never went down. It never went down. Jesus did this?" I said, "Absolutely." She asked, "How do you know it was Jesus?" That was simple to answer, "Because He left His signature." She asked, "What is that?" I said, "He never gives us just enough. He always gives us exceedingly, abundantly more than we could hope or imagine, and that is His signature." Within the next few weeks, that woman gave her life to Jesus. She and her husband now attend a church in Texas, and they are serving the Lord. That is how God works.

Let's circle back around the end of Acts 4:31; the Bible says that the place where they were praying was shaken. Children of God, when we get our courage and boldness together, and start moving in the power of the Holy Spirit, the nation will shake under the power of God. The nation will shake when the Church stops walking with a limp and starts running the way it is supposed to run. The Church will have revival, and the world will have an awakening. That is how we are supposed to operate.

Love Jesus More

The Spirit of the Lord is doing a work within the Church of America. He is shaking up the ground, and the Remnant people have begun to rise up. There is a hunger in the post-pandemic Church for the courts of the Living God. The post-pandemic Church has done away with traditional American Christianity and has embraced the fact that King Jesus is coming; they are preparing their lives for His return. It is so powerful, and what is more exciting is that young people are rising up with it. These young people love Jesus and want to serve God. They just want an authentic move and do not want our legalistic boxes. They want the power of God. They want what is authentic. And you know what? So do I.

I want an authentic move of God's Spirit. God is doing a great thing among His people. God is raising up a people in these last days and preparing an army for His return. It is an exciting time to be a believer, and if you feel otherwise, let me help you today. We might be the minority, but "If God be for us, who can be against us?" We may appear outnumbered, but with God, we never are.

I was preaching at a youth rally in a very urban part of New York. with some tough kids in attendance. Those tough kids folded their arms during most of the worship with a posture of *entertain me*. I preached, and when I gave the altar call, those tough kids lifted their hands in an act to give their lives to Jesus. "Come up," I encouraged, but they would not come up at first. So I said, "Have the courage to come up to this altar. You have all the courage in the world to stand for the world, now have the same courage and come stand for the Lord." I do not ask people to close their eyes and bow their heads during altar calls. If you cannot walk up to the front and give your life to Jesus in a room full of people who will celebrate it, you will never stand in a world that is against you. So I continued, "I want every eye opened, every head up, and if you want to accept the Lord Jesus, come up here now." And those tough kids came up and genuinely gave their lives to Jesus.

Let me share a testimony from our online prayer sessions (please refer to the intro for more information on when and where we meet). This testimony is about one of my spiritual sons. I have known him since he was fourteen years old. He is now a husband and father. While driving home one day, he felt a massive pain in the back of his neck. Suddenly, he started experiencing double-vision and was overcome with projectile vomiting. He is a doctor, so he automatically knew what it was. Once he arrived at the hospital, he told the medical staff what was happening. He said, "There is bleeding in my brain," and they immediately brought him into the ER to be evaluated. I called on the prayer ministry the moment I was notified, and they began to pray.

The doctors had to perform a procedure on his brain to determine where the bleeding was coming from. However, the procedure required the use of a dye that he is allergic to, and there was no other alternative. Using this dye consequently shut down his kidneys.. Shortly after the procedure, the doctors diagnosed him with pneumonia, and he was put on a ventilator. You might be wondering, *And the bleeding?* They still hadn't found it. Then, all of a sudden, his heart stopped working properly, and one right after the other, every organ began to fail, but we continued to pray.

And as we continued, the Lord showed me a vision of a dragon circling his bed. I stood with this ministry against this dragon that was coming. It was the spirit of death, and we stood and prayed. The medical professionals were monitoring him, and all of a sudden, everything stopped. He coded in the middle of the night. But to God's glory, the doctor in charge of the code team just happened to be in the room. My spiritual son was down for five minutes. When they finally got him back, they were unclear about the damage that might have been done. It was five minutes without oxygen. But when he woke up from being sedated, he began correcting the doctors and their choice of medications. He used a chalkboard to communicate as he was still on the ventilator. He questioned, "Why are you giving me this? You should be giving me this!" Amazing right?! His mind was fully functional! More tests were still being run, and it was touch and go for a long time. But I remember visiting him, and I told him, "There is an army praying for you 24 hours a day. Listen to me; this is not your story. This is just a chapter. The story is going to be your testimony."

Well, family, I am happy to report he is home now. He is back at work and is doing well. We continued to pray for complete healing, but God rescued him from death. I asked him if he remembered anything when he coded."You know, it's funny. I saw a dragon coming for my life, but I felt that there was just a protection over my life." You know what that was, family? It was the prayers of the saints. Do not ever underestimate the power of prayer. Prayer becomes a force field against the power of darkness. It is our strength. We have the ability to hold off the things of darkness and say, *No, no, no. We know who we are. We know what the Word of God says and will stand in our authority. Amen!*

Remnant people, I have already referred to the Church, 'us' as the Remnant for multiple reasons. In 2020, God made it very clear that there would be a clear divide. In America today, 70% of people call themselves Christians. Of that 70%, 55% say, I do not have to follow Jesus to be a Christian. I want you to hear that again. Of the 70% that say they are Christians, 55% say they do not have to follow Jesus to be a Christian.

I do not know who they are following then because the only way to be a Christian is to follow Jesus. That is, by definition, what a Christian is: a follower of Christ. Labeling oneself a Christian does not make one a Christian. Half the stars in Hollywood will tell you they are Christians. But do their lives speak of the gospel? It is not your words that speak of the gospel: it is your very life that should speak of it.

I want you to get used to hearing the word Remnant because that is who God is raising up in this hour. I say it so that we get used to it. And I say it because I am prophetically calling it out. Let God raise up a Remnant people.

There are many markers of the Remnant people. Four that stand out to me are as follows: 1. To be holy, 2. To love the Lord, 3. To yield to the Word of God, 4. To make Jesus the most precious being in your life. The corrupt church will use the Bible and many other resources to advance their agenda. But for the Remnant people, the Bible is the only thing we use. There is no comparison to the Bible. The Bible is where I subject my life.

There should be nothing more valuable to us than King Jesus. Isn't that a given? Is it? The answer is, *No!* Because we love a lot of things. And when push comes to shove, we have to ask ourselves, *is Jesus the most precious being to me?*

Revelation 12:10-11 tell us, "Then I heard a loud voice saying in heaven, "Now salvation, and strength, and the kingdom of our God, and the power of His Christ have come, for the accuser of our brethren, who accused them before our God day and night, has been cast down. And they overcame him by the blood of the Lamb and by the word of their testimony, and they did not love their lives to the death." Often, when we quote these verses, we refer to just two parts, "...they overcame by the blood of the Lamb and by the word of their testimony," but the Bible gives us a third part, "...and they did not love their lives unto death." There is a third way that you overcome as a Remnant people.

To overcome, you must not love your lives unto death. Did you read that? In other words, Jesus should be more precious than your very life. Now, we can take this literally like the martyrs and the persecuted church right. There is no group of people that I honor and respect more than the persecuted church. If you are unaware, there is persecution happening in this world for the gospel of Jesus Christ. The year 2015 to the present day is considered the greatest era of persecution in church history. Yes, from 2015 until now, not even the Roman era matches what is going on now. The greatest persecution is going on now for the gospel of Jesus Christ.

People are giving their lives for Jesus. The three fastest-growing churches in the world are in Iran, China and Afghanistan. Yes, Iran, China, and Afghanistan. Do you know what happens to these people if they are caught preaching the gospel? They are executed. And they are executed publicly to stop others from preaching the gospel. But do you know what it actually does? It incites people. Do you understand that these parents are teaching their children how to die? *Pray this prayer if you are caught and make sure to repent for your sins before they kill you.* They live every single day, every moment, with this potential scenario. The Taliban ravishes Afghanistan, door to door to door, and yet the church is exploding.

In fact, they do not have enough people in Iran to baptize new believers because people are getting saved quickly. People are just jumping in a pool and baptizing themselves because they are having encounters with the King of Kings and the Lord of Lords. He is speaking to them. And these Christians are living the Word; they do not love their lives unto death. They love Jesus more than their lives, and they speak that way. They say *we know that at any moment, we can be with Jesus.* They live on the edge of that at every moment. Shame on the American Christian. The moment we are uncomfortable, we want to go home. I have pastored churches for many years; believe me, I know. *Pastor, it's too hot in here. Pastor, it's too cold in here. Pastor, I don't like this song. Pastor, I'm not happy with this.* I heard it all the time.

I grew up in New York City. I am a Brooklyn girl. At nineteen, I went to Bible school, and they sent me to work at Plymouth Rock Assembly of God. The pilgrim's Plymouth Rock. I was from Brooklyn. Do you know how ridiculous that was? They basically sent me to a foreign country. I walked into the church, and worship was with a banjo. I was like, "Am I in a movie? What is happening?" I went to the Pastor's house after church for dinner. My beautiful mom raised me right. So I asked the Pastor's wife if I could help with dinner. "Absolutely; why don't you get the string beans?" I opened the refrigerator. She looked and laughed, "What are you doing?" "I'm getting the string beans." "Not there." So I opened the freezer because where else would string beans be except the refrigerator or the freezer? "Oh, honey, no, no, outside." "Outside? You want me to go pick string beans?" I went. I then turned around and said, "Lord, I'll get the string beans, but if they want milk for their coffee, they are on their own. I'm not doing that."

They sent me to a country church where worship was with a banjo, and you know what I did every Sunday? I worshiped. It does not matter if it is with a banjo or a song I like or anything at all! But as American Christians, we are so used to being catered to. So much so that we have become consumers instead of disciples. We need to learn from those giving their lives for the gospel, who cannot even raise their voice when they worship because someone might hear them. They would love to sing out loud. They would love to lift their hands. They would love to own an entire Bible. May we learn from them. May we learn from their lives, those who give their lives daily for the gospel. We can look at it literally, but there is something else I want you to learn from this. Often, the Bible is multi-dimensional. It has multiple meanings. In this passage from Revelations, the writer is talking about not loving their lives unto death, not just physically, but also about another death.

The death inside us, the death to our ways, the death to our thinking, the death to our ambition, the death to our dreams, and the death to the things we want and desire. Are any of these things bad? No. But we have a mentality as Americans that we must keep acquiring stuff. We need a savings account. We need a 401K. We need to make sure we have the best promotion. We have to be CEO. We keep getting and getting and getting, and these things become precious to us. They become valuable to us, and they, in themselves, are not the issue. The issue is that they become so valuable to us that Christ is not first. The death inside of us, as a Remnant people, is that we live our life surrendered, and automatically all those other things are on the table.

We love to acquire things because it makes us feel secure. We want to make sure we have a good retirement so we will be okay in the future. We fail to understand that all we need is a good God. That does not mean that we are careless. It does not mean that we do not do the right thing. What it means is that our trust is not in earthly things. Any one of these things can be taken away, and we will still be okay. Any one of these things can be moved, and we will be okay. I promise you that when we acquire these things and hold them as precious, those things hold us. I resigned with nothing when I left my pastoral position. My prayer was that my faith would release faith in the room. From that day, we had multiple families leave the church because God had been calling them to move somewhere else for years, and they had previously refused. When we hold things as precious, they hold us back and keep us trapped. What happens when I think I must have this job, when I must have this education, when I hold these things precious? Maybe God is saying, *I have a different route for you,* and you must learn to lean into it.

Will you surrender to that route? If the Lord were to speak to you today and say, *I want you to empty your bank account,* how would that sit with you? *I want you to quit your job today. I want you to give away your car. I want you to walk away from this position.* How would any of that sit with you? Because when I love Jesus as the most precious being in my life, there is nothing more valuable than that. He can touch anything He wants in my life because I have acknowledged that He is God and I am not.

Success can be very dangerous because you can succeed at something God never called you to do. You can be successful at something that God never called you to do, and then, in the end, your success will not matter. Your treasure is not on this Earth. I have done enough funerals, I promise you. Everyone leaves exactly the same, with the clothes on their back and their spirit either in heaven or hell. And that is the end of it. Nothing else goes with us, so you better make sure you have stored up for yourself treasure in heaven. You can be successful, yet success can be deceitful because you have succeeded at something God never called you to do. You can be the best doctor, but if Jesus did not call you to be a doctor, guess what? It does not matter. You could be the best banker, with awards covering your wall, but if He did not call you to do that, it means nothing in eternity. You want to be successful at what He has called you to do. You want to be faithful in what He has called you to do. Believe me, you can store up all the treasure you want on Earth, and it will not matter. Our treasure is in heaven.

In Luke 12:13, we read a parable, "Then one from the crowd said to Him, "Teacher, tell my brother to divide the inheritance with me." But He said to him, "Man, who made Me a judge or an arbitrator over you?" And He said to them, "Take heed and beware of covetousness, for one's life does not consist in the abundance of things he possesses." Then He spoke a parable to them: "The ground of a certain rich man yielded plentifully. And he thought within himself, saying, 'What shall I do, since I have no room to store my crops?' So he said, 'I will do this: I will pull down my barns and build greater, and there I will store all my crops and my goods. And I will say to my soul, "Soul, you have many goods laid up for many years; take your ease; eat, drink, and be merry."' But God said to him, 'Fool! This night your soul will be required of you; then whose will those things be which you have provided?' So is he who lays up treasure for himself, and is not rich towards God."

This man has many things. He has gathered many things. He is prepared for the future, but that night his life was required of him. When I get to heaven, I do not want a list of the things I did not do. I want to get to heaven and have God say; *You obeyed me in everything I asked. Here are the souls that are here because of your life.* And I do not know about you, but everything is on the table for me. The life of a Remnant person is not holding things with a closed fist. We do not hold on to our things, not even our ministries, because they are not ours. We do not build God's house. That is a fallacy. Jesus said *I build My house. I build My house, and the gates of hell do not prevail against it.* We do not build God's house. He allows us to walk beside Him as He does, but He builds His own house. Those who are living Remnant lives do not hold anything close: not their careers, not their jobs, not their finances, nothing, not even their lives. Nothing is held with a closed fist. Everything is held open-handed.

Open your hands. What does that mean? It means that nothing is more precious than You, Jesus, nothing. Until my death, nothing is more precious. My hands are open. That is why we worship with our hands open. It is a symbol of our hearts being open. *Lord, touch whatever You want and require of me. Whatever You want, I trust You. My hands are open.* And let me tell you, you can never out-honor God. When you live with your hands open, God also lives with His hands open. That is the response of God. When He has people who trust Him that much and say, *God, everything is on the table*, God says, *great, and everything from heaven is at your feet. I will make a way for you.* Hear the testimonies of the persecuted church. Hear their testimonies. They are living in Elijah days. There are birds coming to feed them. You have no idea of their testimonies. Muslims have shown up at their doors because the Holy Spirit showed them a picture of Jesus. Not knowing who Jesus was, these Muslims received a vision of an address and a voice saying *go, and they will tell you who I am.* When you live open-handed, God pours out His blessing into it. When you live saying, *God, everything is on the table*, things happen.

I have one of my spiritual daughters who moved to California. She is a little firecracker, and she lives with open hands. That is why she is there. The Lord showed her this homeless community and said, "I want you to prepare packages for them." She had just started working as a student-teacher for a Christian school, and when God gave her this instruction, she had just about used all her funds. Still, she obeyed the Lord and emptied what was left in her account. She made the packages even though she didn't have money for rent. She didn't even have food for the following week. She just obeyed the Lord and lived open-handed.

On the day she gave out the packages, the school's principal asked to speak with her. "The testimony of your teaching has filled this school. Everyone is talking about this teacher from New Jersey. You have blown away the students, and you have blown away the other teachers. And because of that, we have decided to give you a $20,000 raise." She had only been there three weeks! Do you know anyone who receives a $20,000 raise after three weeks? Three weeks and then a $20,000 raise. Why? Because she lives with open hands. Nothing to her is more precious than Jesus. As a result, an open heaven now floods her life, and she walks in the supernatural. Why? Because God responds to us living like this. But when you hold things tightly, you block your own blessing.

You block your own blessing when you hold things tightly. *God, not this. Don't touch my savings, God. I worked really hard for that. I worked really hard for this.* God says, *You can have it, and I will keep what I have for you too.* This verse talks about people not looking to store up their comfort and whose security is in the Lord. They do not love their lives unto death. Jesus is so precious to them; they are so in love with Him that they would give their very lives.

One of the pleasures of being a revivalist is seeing different churches. I had the joy of preaching in a storefront church in rural PA. This church was like nothing you have ever seen. It had about 40 people, and the majority were adults with special needs and veterans with traumatic brain injuries. The pastor starts carpooling at around 7 in the morning because most of the congregants have no form of transportation. Each one of these church members is given a special place in this church where they are loved and honored. They come with so many needs, but they also come with so much faith. I was truly blown away by the faith that was in this church. Their pastor has taught them well. The service was amazing, nothing like you would see on the internet. Worship by a musical standard was a disaster, but by a heavenly standard, it was perfect. The altar was filled at the end with hungry souls, and they prayed with all their hearts to the Lord. One moment that will forever be in my heart was when one of the young veterans wanted to read the Bible out loud to the church. You may say, *what is the big deal about that?* Due to his brain injury, he lost his ability to read. As he asked to read, the pastor left the platform, sat next to this young man, and fed him every word so he could Speak the Word of God. It was so beautiful. I told the pastor that this church makes Jesus smile. It is a church to the least of these, people that other churches may overlook, but you have made a home of faith for them. It was a picture of a pastor that wanted nothing more than to please Jesus. He said it is not very glamorous and always a sacrifice, but he simply loves Jesus. He lacks nothing because Jesus provides for all he needs. He could have wanted many easier and more rewarding things, but his reward is not here on earth. He has not loved his life more than Christ; his desires are now God's. Truly an incredible picture of Jesus being his security.

We, as His people, need to learn that it is not anything but the Lord giving us security. It is about Jesus being our complete security. It is not our finances, it is not our education, and it is not our titles. All those things mean nothing in eternity. They mean nothing. What matters is what I have stored up in heaven. What matters is how open-handed I have lived so God can meet my life. I want to challenge you today to live as the Remnant people who are overcome by the blood of the Lamb and by the word of their testimony and who do not love their lives unto death. The

Remnant are willing to die for the Gospel of Jesus Christ, both physically and spiritually.

Pray with me!

God, I know You are preparing a people, and I am one of them. Prepare me, God. Prepare me in this hour and at this time to stand for You. Lord Jesus, I do not want to hold anything tighter than I hold You. So today, Lord God, I unclench my hands in an act of faith and say, I will not love my life; I will not love my life more than I love You. I release my faith, my trust today, and I unclench my hands, King Jesus. Everything is on the table. I will not love my life unto death! You are more precious! Amen.

A CHURCH OF POWER

The Church of Jesus Christ should be filled with the power and the anointing of the Holy Spirit. The Church should be operating in the gifts of the spirit. If I were to pick one topic to preach, that is what I would preach on for the rest of my life. I truly believe it is my calling to be an igniter for the Church and to see the church be the Church. That is my heart. This topic burns within me; if I could scream something every day, it would be this; to see the Church be what Jesus died for. I don't know the Church any other way. I was wrecked really early for the kingdom. I saw my first miracle when I was eight years old, and it wrecked me. I saw a limb grow in front of my eyes. A woman had massive back pain and all kinds of issues. She even had special shoes made for her. I watched an evangelist pray for her, and her leg shot out. I was wrecked. The second miracle was when I was eleven years old. I accompanied someone to a hospital visit. A woman had cancer, and it was visible on her neck. As we prayed, I watched it vanish. I was wrecked. I wanted to go through every hospital room and ICU and empty them. Can I tell you I have not changed? That is still my heart.

That is the Church I know. That is what I understand the Church to be. That is the Church Jesus built. Jesus did not build a Church of words. That would be a lecture hall and not a Church. He didn't build a place of debate; that would be a classroom. He built a Church of power. How do we know that? We know because He told the disciples to wait in the upper room. They had all the information. They had all the lessons, they had the experience, but He knew they weren't ready. He told them to go to the upper room and wait. Wait for what? "For my power, wait for my power." When the power came, God told them to go because they were now ready to be the Church. Prior to this, all they had were just some facts and information. They could be good people, but He didn't call them to be just that. He called them to be the Church. What happened in the upper room is very simple. All their knowledge, information, education, and experience with Jesus were now set on fire, and it was no longer in their head; it was now in their spirit. It was then that the Church was ready to be the Church. You see, Jesus built a Church that looks like him, and Jesus was filled with power. That is where we are now. God is teaching the post-pandemic Church how to be what He intended. To be who we were called to be.

Think about Jesus' life. There was healing, deliverance, miracles, signs and wonders everywhere He went. Why? Because He was filled with the Holy Spirit. It oozed out of Him, and everyone wanted to be around Him. Thousands of people surrounded Him without the need for social media. Think about that for a minute. How did the word spread? It spread by mouth. *Jesus is coming,* people would say. And thousands of people would come. How does that happen without social media or a printing press? Phones didn't exist; the internet hadn't been invented yet. It was His anointing. It was the power of God over Jesus. People went everywhere He went and were healed, delivered, and set free. And then, when the disciples got touched, the same thing happened again. Jesus said, "You will do greater works than I." Why? Because now, there would no longer be just one person filled with the power of the Holy Spirit; there would be millions filled with the power of the Holy Spirit. So what does it look like when a million people become on fire with the power of the Holy Spirit? The church becomes the Church.

We have many buildings with pretty programs and nice things, but they have no power. That is not the Church God intended. It is not the Church that Jesus built, and I'm not interested in being a part of a church that Jesus didn't build. That is called a waste of time. I want to be part of the Church that Jesus built and is rebuilding during our time. The Church that Jesus built was filled with power. It was filled with the movement of the spirit, with signs and wonders, with prophecy, and with the Words of knowledge and wisdom. That is how the Church should look. We keep trying to find new ways to do church. It's a mistake. We keep looking for different strategies and ideas, yet God's Word has already told us what to do. He told us how to build the Church. I'm okay with being relevant. I want to be relevant. I want to speak a language that this world can understand so it can be saved. But I'm not willing to throw the power out to do it.

I am unwilling to change how Jesus desires His Church to be built; I want to move forward according to His instructions and with His power. I'll give you a simple example. I was out for dinner on a particular New Year's Eve with one of my best friends. As we were sitting in the restaurant, I looked across the restaurant and saw this beautiful, regal African American woman, probably in her 70s. She was sitting there all dressed up, but she was by herself. She ordered two meals, two drinks, and a big salad. Something in my heart pulled towards her. I wondered, "Lord, what's her story?" Instantly, He gave me a word of knowledge. He said her husband died this year, and they celebrated New Year's Eve like this every year. This is the first year she's celebrating without him, but she kept their tradition. I asked the Lord what He wanted me to do. He said, "I want you to pay her bill and tell her it's from Me. Tell her, "I know this is your first year without your husband, but you'll never have a year without Me."

I called the waitress over and asked for the woman's bill. I explained what I was doing, and she cried, "Oh, that's amazing," she said between her tears. I told her she needed to stop crying because I didn't want the woman to know it was me. The next thing I know, the manager comes over. Because he's so touched, he wants to bless us and comp our bill. I just wanted everyone to stop drawing attention to us because now I have four waitresses by our table and everyone's crying. But we sent the woman the message God put in my heart. I can't even begin to tell you her reaction. She was elated, teary, emotional and blessed. She couldn't believe that the Lord would reach out to her like that. But He did, and that is what the Church is supposed to do. It is not about what He spoke to me; I was absent. It is not about me but about allowing the Holy Spirit to use me for the kingdom to advance. That woman will never be the same again.

That is not just for me; that is for us, for the Church. The Church is meant to look like that, and anything else is not the Church; everything else is just fun. The Church is about power; the Church is about anointing. The Church is about the move of the Holy Spirit on display. The English preacher Charles Spurgeon said it best, "I don't think the devil cares how many churches are built as long as they are filled with lukewarm pastors and people!" They are no threat to him. However, the church that Jesus built will cause all of hell to shake!

In 1 Corinthians, Paul is writing to the church of Corinth. The Church of Corinth was planted properly. It was a healthy church. While it was planted properly, there came a time when it began to veer off. It began to do things on its own. It began to add things that it shouldn't add. They began to think they knew better, and they began to veer off, much like the Church in America. We've become something else. We've started doing things a little differently than we were supposed to. The Church of Corinth allowed some carnality into the church. Paul writes a letter to them to set them straight and put them in order again. In 1 Corinthians 2:1, he tells them, "And I, brethren, when I came to you, did not come with excellence of speech or wisdom declaring to you the testimony of God. For I am determined not to know anything among you except Jesus Christ and Him crucified. I was with you in weakness, in fear, and in much trembling. And my speech and my preaching were not with persuasive words of human wisdom, but in demonstration of the Spirit and the power, that your faith should not be built in the wisdom of men but in the power of God."

We see that Paul is beginning to adjust the people because they have veered so far away from the things of God. And if I use our vernacular, he said, "I didn't come to you with a bunch of talk. I didn't try to impress you with my words. I didn't come and make some beautiful soliloquy of what I wanted you to do. I came to you with the power and the demonstration of the Holy Spirit. I came to you under the anointing of the Holy Spirit. That is how we started, but you've moved." In verse five, Paul says "that your faith should not be in the wisdom of men but in the power of God." Unfortunately, this is what the Church is guilty of today. We begin to move, build wealth and seek our wisdom. We begin to move in our understanding. We measure everything by what works for us using our rationale and thinking. The Scripture very clearly warns us not to lean on our own understanding and that there is a way that seems right to man but leads to destruction.

We were never supposed to build our faith through our own wisdom and knowledge. Our wisdom is empty. Our wisdom is limited. We think we know everything, but we don't. As we get older, we find out we know less. Then when life throws us five, six, seven, eight, twenty curve balls, we realize we know nothing. Our wisdom is fleeting; that is why our faith is not built on it. We can't use our reasoning; the Scripture says our faith can't be built on it. Faith has to be built on the power of the Holy Spirit. That is the only way faith is built. Faith is not built because you understand faith. Faith is not built because it makes sense. Faith is built on trusting God and walking in what He has.

Man's wisdom and faith in God are polar opposites; they are contrary and at war with one another. Faith, often, doesn't make sense and looks ridiculous. We can look at the stories in the Old Testament and see how faith doesn't always make sense and how it sometimes even looked ridiculous. Everyone loves the story of Goliath falling to the ground, a fabulous ending. Walls of Jericho falling down, another fabulous ending. When we read about these happenings, we see how ridiculous those people looked. Israel had to fight against an army that had never been defeated. A wall that had never been conquered, and they went to battle with a guitar and a flute. Ridiculous. Do you know how ridiculous they looked, singing to the wall? Not one day, but seven, going to war with their guitar and flute. *Lord, we're hungry; we want meat. No problem, go outside. I'm going to rain you down quail.* Fabulous, right? Do you have any idea what that looked like? Put your hand out now; I'm going to drop a chicken. Is that not ridiculous? It's ridiculous! Steps of faith look ridiculous; they don't match your logic because they're not meant to back your logic; they're meant to bypass your logic.

Your logic is subject to faith, not the other way around. Your logic has to surrender under your faith in the Lord. That's how faith grows. But we've changed all that. Now we think the Word has to make sense before it's applied. But it doesn't. We think God's voice has to make sense. No, it doesn't. We just have to obey it; that's it. I grew up in a Church in Staten Island, which was originally relocated from Brooklyn. Pastor Crandall, the senior pastor at that time, received a word from the Lord to move the church from Brooklyn to Staten Island. This was in the early '80s, when Staten Island was known for two things: a swamp and a garbage dump. New York City had a tremendous area, and Staten Island was used as the city's garbage dump. There were also massive areas of swamp land. Pastor Crandall, in obedience, went to Staten Island and God led him to a property on Richmond Avenue. Richmond Avenue had not been developed yet; however, the Lord led him to buy this particular property. He bought it by faith. Everyone told him that it was a mistake. He was told that no one would go to Staten Island, especially not to a place that wasn't developed. They told him he didn't know how to build, as he had never done this before.

But Pastor Crandall knew he had heard the voice of the Lord, so he bought the land. Shortly after, a surveyor was hired (as was part of the process before a build), and he measured the ground. He informed the pastor of a huge problem; he said the church could not be built on that land. The law required the ground to be 12 inches or less deep to build on a swamp. The ground on Richmond Ave was 13 inches deep, and because of that one inch, they would not let him build. "Sorry, but you've been ripped off!" the surveyor said. The church had invested everything it had into this land. So the pastor, because he heard God and was a man of faith, gathered his deacons, elders, and his staff together. He instructed them to call all the members of the church. Keep in mind; this was the early '80s; there was no text or email. Hundreds of phone calls were made to the members. They were instructed to meet at the property on a certain day and time. The entire church came out!

I was a little kid then, and I remember being so excited. I didn't know what was happening, but the pastor had called, so we all ran. When we got there, we held hands around the property and began to pray, "God, you gave us your word." People were laughing while driving by, looking at these ridiculous people. They didn't know what was going on. It looked ridiculous. We were praying and praying. When we finished praying, the pastor said, "Everyone stay here." He called the surveyor and asked him to come back and measure the land. He said, "Sir, I just measured the land." The pastor said, "Come back again; humor me." The surveyor, annoyed that he had to come back, didn't even talk to us. He walked around measuring the land once, twice, three times. We didn't know what was happening. He walked over to us and asked, "What did you guys exactly do here?" "We prayed;

why?" "Well, I measured the land, and it was 13 inches before." "What is it now?" "It's 11; it's 11."

That church still stands today. That church has five satellite churches. It has five services every Sunday, one in Spanish and one in Korean, and it is a massive sending station for missionaries worldwide. Why? Because one man was willing to look ridiculous, one man put his natural mind in check and operated in the spirit. One man, and look what came of it. Child of God, you must learn to put your natural mind in check and allow yourself to walk and operate in the spirit of God. You must begin to know what it looks like to step into the things of God and obey His voice. As you begin to obey His voice, His voice gets louder. He speaks, and you obey. He speaks, and you obey. If He speaks and you don't obey, He won't speak as much.

Parents know what it's like to speak and have no one listen. Go clean your room. Go clean your room. No one is listening. You want someone to listen, and God is the same. God is looking for people who want to walk in the spirit and listen. As you listen, His voice gets clearer because He knows He can trust you. He knows you will honor Him, and He knows you will do what He says.

If you want to begin to operate in the things of the spirit, you need to begin to step out. Salvation is free, everything else requires work. If you want to be a man or woman of the spirit, it requires work. If you want to be a giant in the kingdom, it requires work. He already gave you salvation for free. He is not going to give you everything else. You have to get to work. You have to get on your knees. You have to begin to step into the things of the spirit.

The first thing you need to do is begin to create room for the Holy Spirit. He is a gentleman. The Holy Spirit shows up when we make room for Him. Is it not silly to ask Him to show up but not give Him room? We ask him to show up; then, we must create the room.

The Holy Spirit is much more important than anything else and making room has to become part of your life. You have to start creating. If you want the gifts of the spirit, if you want God to begin to use you, if you want prophecy and to see miracles, then you must begin to create room for those things. Many Christians think that if God wants to give them gifts, He'll just give them, but that is not Scripture. Scripture says, "Seek, ask, knock. Seek, ask, knock." He's looking for you to begin to ask Him and to begin to seek Him out. God, I want to be used by you. I want your gifts. If the Holy Spirit does not baptize you, ask Him for it. It is His good pleasure to baptize you, and if you've been baptized in the Holy Spirit, don't stop there. Just being baptized in the Holy Spirit and not going further is like putting the keys in the car, turning on the car but not going anywhere. There's a ride to take. Begin to ask for other things. I want to move in prophecy, God. I want to move in miracles, God. Begin to ask for these things so that you can be the Church.

Begin to create room in your life for the Holy Spirit. Turn off the phone, turn off the TV, and all these things that distract you. Even close some of your books. Some of you love to read, and that's fine, but spend time with Him, too. Sit in His presence. I ask Him all day, Holy Spirit, have Your way, have Your way, have Your way. When you ask Him to have His way, He does.

Once you begin to make room, begin to surrender deeper regularly. What do you surrender? Your will, your ambition, your pride, your reputation. We don't surrender because we don't want to look foolish, and someone might see us. On a trip back home from Mexico, I was in the Guadalajara airport banging on the gate door because I almost missed my flight back home; I looked ridiculous. Everybody in the waiting room was looking at the crazy woman banging on the window, and then all of them were silenced when the crew opened the plane for me. You have to be willing to be ridiculous. You have to be willing to surrender your will, your thought process, and the way you think. Am I willing to surrender that to the Lord? Am I willing to allow God to have that space in my thinking, ambition, and pride? Am I willing to be foolish for the kingdom's sake?

Am I willing to look ridiculous for the kingdom's sake? Am I willing to do things that other people might question so that God can show off? The Bible tells us that He uses the foolish things of the world to confound the wise. He used the guitar and a flute to knock down the wall at Jericho. He used a little shepherd boy with a rock to kill a giant. He used a bunch of people that have never been to war to conquer everything. He parts the Red Sea because a man stood with a stick. I want you to read that again, Moses is standing with a stick over the Red Sea. That's a ridiculous picture until the sea parted. Until the sea parted, it wasn't ridiculous after that, and you have to be willing to ridiculously surrender and make room for God to do a work in you and through you.

Are you willing to step out and be obedient to what God says? Are you willing to step out and let God have His way in you and through you? Are you willing today for God to speak and then obey? My desire is for you to say, *I'll do what you say, God, no matter how ridiculous I look. I'm willing to step out. I want more of You. I want my faith to be built on the power of the Holy Spirit and I don't want the wisdom of man. I want to be a spirit-filled and spirit-empowered person.*

As we end this chapter, pray with me:

We refuse to be average or complacent. We refuse just to be good Christians, Lord God. We want to be the Church on fire. We want to be the men and women you've called us to be, Lord God. We want to be filled with you. We want to be the Church that You built, Jesus. We don't want to be anything else. We're not interested in being anything else. We want your gifts on display so that Your Name can be made famous. We want Your power flowing, Jesus. We surrender our wisdom and we surrender our understanding. Lord, we don't want to be wise in our own eyes; we want to be wise in your eyes. We want our faith built on the power of Your spirit and not on the wisdom of man. Lord God, we don't want to be convinced by persuasive words but by the power of Your spirit.

Holy Spirit, would you have your way over us, pour over us. We're making room for you Holy Spirit; we're making room for you. We surrender everything to You the best way we know how and we're asking you to fill every compartment in us. With every part of our being, we want to be the Church on fire for you. We want to be anointed from head to toe, Lord God. We want to reflect you, Jesus. We want your gifts because we want people to be set free. We want your gifts because we want to see your power flow. We want to see the sick healed, Lord God. We want to see You move. Release Your gifts over Your people, in the Name of Jesus, Amen.

DEEP ROOTS

There are two types of prophecy: the kind that brings revelation and is not known, and the kind that is meant to take deep roots for preparation. In this chapter, we will look at the latter, deep roots for preparation.

I believe God is very direct in what He is saying to us. The answer this world needs is revival, and you can see, I've dedicated this entire book to helping you understand that. The world needs a revival of salvation. The Church needs a revival of power. We need revival. It is not a want; it is not an ask; it is the answer to an act of desperation. We need revival.

There is a story in First Samuel that I love so much and speaks to what we are facing today. The Philistines steal the Ark of the Covenant and take it to where they are. They take the Ark of the Covenant, a symbol of God's presence, and put it overnight inside the temple of their god, Dagon. They specifically place it behind Dagon and go to sleep. When they wake up the next morning, Dagon is on his face! So they pick up Dagon, put him back up, and leave. When they return the next day, Dagon is on the floor again! But this time, his head is severed, his hands are broken, and nothing is left but his torso. God was making a point. *Everything will bow to Me. And if you don't understand that, I'll sever the head of your god and break his hands to make My point.* However, they still don't move the Ark of the Covenant. Shortly after, the Philistines start getting tumors all over their bodies. They finally realized that God had judged them and that the Ark should be returned. So the Ark was removed and sent back to the temple where it belonged; and once again, the symbol of the presence of God was returned.

That is what God has done with us now. He's allowed everything to fall to the ground. And if we didn't get it, He severed its head and broke its hands. He said, *Now, put My presence back in My House. Get rid of everything else, and let it be My presence and My presence alone.* This shaking is not the crisis; it is the awakening. The crisis is coming. It's not here yet; it's coming. And not one crisis but many. God has allowed us to be shaken so we can get the House and our lives in order.

We watched the Church run from a virus and be paralyzed by what was happening worldwide. In that, God revealed to us that we were not ready. But because of it, God has given us an opportunity to prepare, and to prepare we need revival. What is going to get us ready is the complete understanding that we need God. We need a move of the Spirit. God is changing the face of the Church of America. He is changing it. He is stripping it down to the ground. The idols I have discussed have seeped into every aspect of the Church of America. They've even seeped into our worship. Have you ever realized how many songs we sing about ourselves? About us! How do I feel? Worship isn't about how you feel; worship is about who He is.

It has seeped into our teaching. Grace is not a bad word, nor is grace an excuse. Grace is a remedy. What exactly are you coming to Jesus to do? To have a great life? No, you're coming to Jesus to change your life. You're coming to Jesus to die to your old life and get a new life. But we stopped talking like that. And then we take the Holy Spirit and give Him a time slot. 'Holy Spirit, this is when You are allowed to move in Your House.' Imagine that. Imagine someone comes to your house and tells you what you can and cannot do.

But the Church has done just that; it says to the Holy Spirit, *this is when You can move. If You can fit it between worship and announcements, we'd appreciate that. And don't let the altar call go too long because it's getting late and we're hungry.* I believe this grieves the Holy Spirit. It's God's House, and He is taking back the reins. False teachings have and will continue to be exposed. Because what those false teachings have done is rob people of years of walking with God, and God is saying "NO MORE."

I heard an interview from a high-end celebrity about how he had been surrounded by pastors all his life, and he said: "All those pastors with big names, not one of them called me on my junk. They were afraid to. So one day, I found this small storefront church, and I walked in, and the pastor didn't know who I was. I started talking to this pastor about my life. And the pastor ate me alive, in love. The pastor said, 'You need to get your stuff in order, man.' And that moment changed my life." That is how God works. God is stripping away all this fake grace expression. Grace is a tool for me to become more like Jesus; not stay in my sin. We have changed; *Come as you are, to, stay as you are.* No. Come as you are and walk in the door. It doesn't matter if you're broken, hurt, or whatever. Walk in the door. We will welcome you. We will embrace you. We will love you. But we'll love you and instruct you to be more like Jesus. We'll not love you to stay broken, hurt, and in sin. We have failed as the Church if we do that. So come in any way that you are, but change every day.

We know the end from the beginning. We know that we will be a victorious people. But that doesn't mean we're not going to walk through trials and difficulties. We need to begin to comprehend; that as the people of God, victory belongs to the House of God. Jesus and the word victory are synonymous words. It might require a push; it might require a press. It doesn't matter. We are still a victorious people.

We are very familiar with a story found in Daniel, Chapter 3. The people of God, the Israelites, all five million, are taken captive in Babylon. The Babylonians are full of sin, full of idolatry, full of immorality, and full of arrogant, narcissistic kings. King Nebuchadnezzar loves himself so much that he makes a golden statue of himself and puts it right on top of the highest point in their city. He tells the people that when anyone hears the harps, the flute, the guitar, or any kind of music, everyone is to drop whatever they're doing, kneel and worship this idol.

This happens multiple times a day, and everyone is supposed to drop and worship this statue. Some of his men came to him and told him that there were three Jews who had never kneeled. In Daniel 3:8, we read, "Therefore at that time certain Chaldeans came forward and accused the Jews. They spoke and said to King Nebuchadnezzar, Oh King, live forever. You, O king, have made a decree that everyone who hears the sound of the harp, flute, lyre, and psaltery, in symphony with all kinds of music, shall fall down and worship the gold image; and whoever does not fall down and worship shall be cast into the midst of a burning fiery furnace. There are certain Jews whom you have set over the affairs of Babylon: Shadrach, Meshach, and Abednego; These men, O King, have not paid due respect to you. They do not serve your gods or worship the golden image which you have set up."

"Then Nebuchadnezzar, in rage and fury, gave the command to bring Shadrach, Meshach, and Abednego. So they brought these men before the king. Nebuchadnezzar spoke to them, "Is it true Shadrach, Meshach, and Abednego, that you do not serve my gods and worship the gold image which I have set up? Now, if you are ready, at the time you hear the sound of the horn, flute, harp, lyre, and psaltery, in symphony with all kinds of music, and you fall down and worship the image which I have made, good!"

"But if you do not worship, you shall be cast immediately into the midst of a burning fiery furnace. And who is the God who will deliver you from my hands? Shadrach, Meshach and Abednego answered and said to the king, "O Nebuchadnezzar, we have no need to answer you in this matter. If that is the case, our God whom we serve is able to deliver us from the burning fiery furnace, and He will deliver us from your hand. But if not, let it be known to you, O king, that we do not serve your gods, nor will we worship the golden image which you have set up." Then Nebuchadnezzar was full of fury, and the expression on his face changed toward Shadrach, Meshach and Abednego. He spoke and commanded that they heat the furnace seven times more than usual. And he commanded certain mighty men of valor, who were in his army, to bind up Shadrach, Meshach and Abednego, and cast them into the burning fiery furnace. Then these men were bound in their coats, trousers, turbans, and other garments, and were cast into the midst of the burning fiery furnace. Therefore, because the king's command was urgent, the furnace exceedingly hot, the flame of the fire killed those men who took Shadrach, Meshach and Abednego."

"And these three men, Shadrach, Meshach and Abednego, fell down and were bound in the midst of the burning fiery furnace. Then the king Nebuchadnezzar was astonished; and he rose in haste and spoke, saying to his council, 'Did we not cast three men bound into the midst of the fire?' They answered and said, 'True, O king.' 'Look!' he answered, 'I see four men loose, walking in the midst of the fire; and they are not hurt and the form of the fourth is like the Son of God.'"

I love this story. It is so wild it almost sounds like a fairy tale. But this legitimately happened. The king makes an idol and commands everyone to worship it. Three decide not to worship and are brought before the king. The king gives them another chance. The next time they hear the trumpets and the harp, they are to fall down and worship; that would make everything right. And the king asked them for an answer.

They replied, stating they would not serve nor bow down to his god. And if the punishment for that is to be thrown in the furnace, their God would rescue them. And even if He didn't rescue them, they would not worship. And Nebuchadnezzar becomes so enraged that his whole face changes. He ties them up. He makes the furnace seven times hotter and commands his men to take them immediately to be thrown into the furnace. The men who threw them in are burnt and killed. Nebuchadnezzar went immediately to see if they were dead, and he was astonished. In the vernacular, he says, "Wait, wait, wait, wait. How many men did we throw in? They said, 'We threw in three.' He said, 'But why are there four? And why are they walking around freely? And the fourth one has the form of the Son of God." He removes them, and they don't even smell like smoke. How many of you cook a meal and smell your meal all day? But they're in the fiery furnace and don't even smell like smoke. It's an incredible story.

I want to look into this story further because these three Remnant men left markers for us to learn from. There are markers for us; markers that we need to experience, that we need to get right, to be prepared for our furnaces, for the things coming our way. The first one has to do with their incredible allegiance to God. They knew where their allegiance belonged. There are two things that the Church is confused about. Allegiance and identity. These young men knew their allegiance, and they knew their identity. Clearly, they were not confused. The Church today is very confused about both. We are confused about our allegiance, and we are confused about our identity. These young men understood their allegiance was to God and God alone. Our allegiance is to the cross of Jesus Christ.

Our allegiance is to Jesus. And to Jesus alone. He deserves all our loyalty. He deserves all our allegiance. He deserves all of us to stand with Him. That is allegiance. Our allegiance doesn't belong to anyone else or anything else. The only thing that I worship is Jesus. The only thing that I yield my life to is Jesus. The only thing that I bow my knee to is Jesus. The only thing I surrender my life to is Jesus. That is where my allegiance belongs.

Our allegiance is the cross. We must bring people to the cross. Do you want to see racism vanish? Bring them to the cross. Let the power of the cross meet their hearts. Let the power of the cross touch their hearts. You will see black, white, Hispanic, Asian etc; it won't matter. The cross is the equalizer. I don't need anything else but the cross. It's only the cross. I only bow to the cross. I only yield to the cross.

The cross will destroy every other line. You know why people don't think the cross is enough? Because they don't understand the cross. They don't understand the power of the cross. If they understood the power of the cross, their allegiance would be nowhere else. And these young men understood their allegiance to God. They weren't afraid of anyone else. Their allegiance was to the King of Kings and Lord of Lords. And they said *He is our God. We will not bow. He is enough to protect us. He's enough to change us. He's enough to guard us. It is simply God.* But the Church today has divided allegiance. Our allegiance is spread thin in too many places and with too many people. And what happens when you have allegiance everywhere? The allegiance to one is divided.

Take marriage for example. A marriage starts with just two. The couple's time is their time. Then you add kids to the mix, and now they're trying to find time to do what? Everything. This one needs this. This one needs that. And God forbid a parent calls on the other end; they need something. That's what happens when we split our allegiance. Everything gets a little bit of us, and what everyone gets is watered down. I need to tell you that the cross is enough. It deserves our loyalty. It deserves our allegiance. Our allegiance means I swear by that, I am willing to give my life for that. I am willing to die for that right there. I will die for the cross of Jesus Christ, even if it means my death. I'm okay with that because that's where my allegiance stands. These Remnant young men in Daniel chapter 3 showed us that their allegiance was to God.

Another marker for us from their testimony is that of their identity. They knew who they stood for. They knew who they were. The Church today, the Church of Jesus Christ is having an identity crisis. We don't understand who we are. We are confused. A moment in history that was an obvious marker for me was when Ruth Bader Ginsburg died. Don't get offended. I'm just going to be honest. I saw Christians all over blessing her, saying what an icon, what an amazing, amazing woman she was, what a trailblazer and what a legacy she left. And I was confused. Because I'm a woman, I should actually agree with them, but I don't. They're actually wrong. And I'll tell you why. My identity is Kingdom first. I am Kingdom first. My noun in my life, the thing that I am is a Christian. Everything else is an adjective. My being a woman is an adjective. My being Egyptian is an adjective. These descriptors are second to me being a Christian. And if something elevates being a woman more than being a Christian, guess who wins every time?

This woman that everyone is boasting about and praising was the biggest advocate on the Supreme Court for abortion. She was the biggest advocate for late-term abortion. Abortion up to eight months, to be exact. She was the first person in America to perform a homosexual wedding and performed thousands after that. She was solely responsible for removing the words "In the year of our Lord.," from all our legal documents. She fought against religious freedoms. She fought against the Church. So I cannot celebrate her. I won't. I pray she met Jesus and came to know him. I recognize that she did work for women. I don't deny that. But I won't celebrate her because my identity is not in being a woman. My identity is not in being an Egyptian. My identity is not in who I am. My identity is found in the person of Jesus Christ. My identity is found in the kingdom.

Our identity is not found in our ethnicity, color, or our gender; it is found in Jesus. We are not here to represent a political party. Our interests are heaven. So, anyone who advances heaven, I'll celebrate. If you don't advance heaven, I can't celebrate you. I can't join hands with you. And this is where the Church is having an identity crisis. They think their identity is their color, nationality, or gender. That is not your identity. That is your description. We need to get our identity straight. We need to recognize that we should be about the kingdom. We are not here to advance anything else but the kingdom. We are here to move the kingdom forward. We are here to move the cause of Christ forward. And these young men understood that. They understood who they were.

Let us circle back a bit and focus on allegiance. They understood their allegiance, and they understood their identity. Allegiance does not mean you will be the majority. Remember, there were five million Israelites in captivity. That means five million bowed, except for three. Can you imagine what that looked like? Everyone who can be seen bows except for three teenagers, these three young men. They stay standing, and the Remnant (these teens) are willing to stand by themselves because they're standing for Him. There's a weight to that. The Remnant needs to be able to stand by themselves; they need to be able to stand for the cause of Christ when no one else will. They need to be able to speak the truth when no one else does. I have said these things about the Judge and other people/ events that have happened in history, and

I have lost people I love because of it. They are mad at me, and I must be okay with that.

I love them and bless them, but if I am going to be a Remnant people, my interest is the kingdom; my interest is not in being likable, and my interest is not in being patted on the shoulder all the time. Many people want you to conform to what they want, but people who know their identity don't conform. They speak the truth. I am interested in only pleasing the Lord. See, Remnant people, when you know your allegiance and identity, you are not interested in anyone else's pleasure, only God's. You're not interested in making anyone happy but God, and if you happen to make other people happy, wonderful. And if it doesn't, I'm sorry, we must keep going. That is what these young men did; they understood their allegiance, and they understood their identity. There is also something else they had; they had incredible courage. Courage is what the Church lacks today. The Church is confused about allegiance, and identity and is completely lost in the area of courage.

I was on a cruise some time ago with a friend of mine, and I was in the pool. There were many people in the pool, and everyone was talking. I'm just sitting there alone, and I hear this conversation. The conversation is about how much they hate church and how much they hate pastors. There are about twenty of them there, and I start cracking up. I'm thinking, "God, you set me up." I can't leave the pool because everyone's blocking the exits. I am stuck.

So I'm sitting there for about a minute, and I say, "Okay, God." I know what's going to happen. This conversation is going to flip my way, so fill my mouth because I don't know what to say." And finally, one guy turns to me, "Hey, what do you think about what we were saying?" And I started laughing. I said, "You know, this is what I think. Do all of you go to the doctor?" And they go, "Yeah." "Have you ever been to a bad doctor?" "Yeah, of course." I said, "Did you give up on your health because you had a bad doctor? Or did you keep looking around until you found a doctor that you liked, and then you could be treated by him?" "Yes." Then I said, "So why did you guys give up on God because of insufficient pastors or bad churches? Why didn't you keep looking until you found someone that could minister to you so you could grow?"

Silence. I was like, 'Thank you, Jesus." And so the guy turns around, he says, "That's a really good answer. What do you do?" I said, "Oh, I work with people." "Oh, you're an educator." "Sure, we'll go with that. Yeah." He asks, "What way?" I'm like, 'Alright, it's three questions.' I said, "Well, in truth, I'm a pastor." So now everyone has this nervous laugh. "But look, listen, no one has to be nervous, no one has to feel awkward. This is the deal. God, in His sovereignty, put me in this pool at this time, with this conversation, because He loves every single one of you. God wanted to speak to you, so He orchestrated my life so that I'm here. No one has to feel nervous or feel awkward." So now they're all laughing. I continued, "And you guys are telling me you can't find a church anywhere?" "No, no." I asked, "Where do you live, sir?" Each one started telling me where they lived. On cruise ships, there are people from all over the country. I knew of a church for every one of them, within five miles of their house!

I knew a church for every single one of them. See, courage just needs you to step out, and God will fill your mouth, anoint you, and speak through you. He just needs you to be willing to open your mouth; He just needs you to stand. And it might not always turn out to be as favorable as my experience, but that doesn't mean we stop being courageous. On the contrary, we need to become more courageous. We need to begin to speak louder when people are trying to legalize disgusting and ungodly things. The Church cannot be silent; the Church has to be courageous. Those three boys in the book of Daniel knew they did not have to go away to think about their answer. They knew their answer right then. That is the courage the Church needs. Courage unleashes the supernatural. If you want the supernatural move of God in your life, you must start getting some courage. Do you know what you do? You pray for the move of the Spirit; You pray for miracles; You pray for God to move, and then You pray that God removes any situation that might hinder courage.

You might say, *God, don't ever let me be in a dangerous situation, don't ever.* Well, how can He show you a miracle? How can He possibly do it if you pray it all away? *God, don't let anything happen today. Amen.*

How does He show up? Instead, say *God, I'm so grateful that every morning I wake up, I have the grace for whatever is coming. You give me fresh manna every day, and whatever is coming today, You give me the grace for, the power, and the courage to overcome.* And then, whatever comes your way, you have the courage and the anointing for it.

If those young men did not have courage, we wouldn't have the story of the fiery furnace. We wouldn't have Daniel in the lion's den if Daniel didn't stand up to the king. If Joshua didn't stand up to the walls of Jericho, we wouldn't have the story of the walls crumbling. The Philistines wouldn't have been defeated if David didn't stand up to Goliath. And we would not have these stories of courage.

Every single one of them required courage. Every single one required the people of God to say, No, no. We stand. We're not moving, and we're not afraid. We will stand for the Lord; we will stand for what is right. And, we are going to believe in God to show up. The final thing those men had was an incredibly deep relationship with the Lord. Their answers and actions revealed the depths of their relationship. "Our God whom we serve is able to deliver us from the burning fiery furnace, ... but if not, let it be known ...that we do not serve your gods, nor will we worship the gold image which you have set up." Why does that answer give it away? Because they trusted God's heart so much. Whether He saved them or not, it was not a game-changer for their stance. When you say, *God, I'm walking into this battle, but it better end up the way I think. I need it to happen that way.* You know what that's called? That is a lack of trust. When we pray, it's not about getting our answer. It's about trusting His heart because His answer might actually be 'no.' Trust Him and trust His heart.

Four years before I left my pastoral position, I remember conversing with God about being tired. I was working sixty-five hours a week, running pounds of ministry, and I was exhausted. I had this conversation with God; I said, "God, I'm tapping out. I'm tired. I'm like the Navy SEAL who wants to ring the bell. Ding, ding, ding." I waited for God to encourage me and speak to my heart. And this is what he said to me, "You can do that. You can tap out. I bless you; I won't leave you, or you can wait and do it my way, and I'll bless you more. You decide." Of course, I wanted to be blessed more; I would be a fool to pass up the more.

And I said, "Okay, God." He instructed me to wait, and four years later, when I left, it was the most beautiful, blessed month I have ever had. It was extraordinary. It was so blessed. God was so in it. When you have a deep relationship with the Lord, you don't have to worry about the outcome because you trust His heart. You trust His character. Just like those young men knew God could save them from the furnace. But if He didn't, they were still not going to bow. Why? Because they trusted Him; they trusted His heart. We need to trust Him, trust His heart.

As Remnant people, you must have a deep relationship with the Lord. You cannot be a casual Christian. You cannot have a casual relationship; you can't even have a friendly relationship. You must have a deep walk with the Lord. Remnant people have deep walks, and they show up in crisis. Pastor Ben Crandall was the president of Zion Bible College, where I attended. He was also the pastor of the church where grew up. He was raised in the depression and had ten brothers and sisters. When he was a little boy, his father had enough of the struggle and left them. His mother now had all these children to raise. She had no income. But she loved Jesus and prayed for everything. Brother Crandall would always tell this story of when he was about seven years old. His mother said, "Okay, boys, everybody, set the table for dinner." They would all look because there was no food on the stove and no food in the refrigerator. "I told you to set the table." So they'd start setting the table while she just walked around praying. "What are we setting at the table? There's no food." "Okay, everyone, come to the table.

We are going to pray for the meal." So all the children sat down and stared at their mom like she was crazy. "Everyone fold your hands, close your eyes. We are going to pray."

"Father, I thank you that you are a God who provides." And she would pray out this beautiful prayer and say 'Amen.' The second she said 'Amen,' she told Benjamin, "open the door for dinner." So he went to the door, opened it, and there would be groceries and food cooked for them, waiting for them right there. "Bring in dinner; God has provided."

People who have a deep relationship with the Lord live in the supernatural. They live in the prophetic. They live in the signs and wonders. Why? Because they have such a deep trust that God is going to show up and God is going to do what He does best. They're not putting God in a box saying, God, you have to only show up this way. Only babies do that. Babies say *God, you can only show up this way.* Mature believers say *God, show up in any way You want. You are God. And I trust You. I trust Your hand, but I trust Your heart even more. And I believe You will meet me.* Remnant people have that deep trust. Remnant people have great courage. Remnant people understand who they are in God, and Remnant people have an allegiance to the cross and the cross alone.

Reckless Obedience

Praying this over you!

Lord, there is no room for babies anymore. There is no more room for half-stepping, God. There is no such thing as a lukewarm believer. You said You would spit them out. It is either hot or cold. There is no in-between. Lord, we declare we want to be hot. And so, Lord, do a work in us. Let Your Word wash us. Let Your Word ignite us. Let us be Your people. We recognize the mantle on us, God; we are the hope of the world. We know it. We recognize it and we receive that mantle with joy. We need your anointing. We need more of You. So, Lord, I pray that everything in us will decrease and You increase. Let everything else be pressed down, and You be raised up. Let everything be pushed to the ground, and Your Name be lifted up in our lives. Make us Your people. Let them look at us and see You; let Your name be glorified. May signs and wonders follow our lives. May we remember that Your Word is not a history book, it is a blueprint. It is not here to tell us about what You used to do. It is here to ignite us for what You are doing. Lord, raise us up and speak to us; let the anointing of Daniel rest upon Your Church so that even in the midst of our Babylon, we can say we know You. Amen.

Do you know that you are blessed and highly favored? We have to remember that we are blessed and highly favored. God's Hand rests upon His people. We are a chosen generation, a royal priesthood.

God is for us. It doesn't matter what is coming against you; just know what is for you. There's something about how we perceive things that cause us to live a little differently. If I understand that it doesn't matter who is coming for me and that it just matters who is with me, then it doesn't matter what or who comes. God is for me! Amen?

The hope of the world is the local church. A local church on fire for the kingdom of Jesus Christ. We need to understand that God is doing a work in the local church and we need to be completely invested because we are the hope of the world. As a revivalist, I travel and preach, and I see Remnant people rising up all over. I've preached in Pennsylvania, South Jersey, New York, etc., and God is doing a work in His people; it's tremendous. A hunger is rising, and my prayer is that it becomes unquenchable.

My prayer is that this hunger becomes unquenchable and that it continues to grow and grow. Over the years, I've learned that hunger is contagious. You get around someone hungry for the things of God, and suddenly, you become hungry for the things of God. In Scripture, it says that God gave the gospel to the Gentiles so that Israel would be jealous. God was strategic. If the Gentiles didn't want it, He would make them want it and by giving the gospel to someone else. He gave the gospel to the Gentiles; which in return, made the Jews jealous. Hunger is contagious. And we are seeing that hunger spread. I am so excited about what God is doing and continues to do.

One aspect that is growing greatly in the Church is prayer. Jesus said, "It is written, 'My house shall be called a house of prayer.'" Not a house *with* prayer, but a house *of* prayer. There is a big difference. A house with prayer means I pray on occasion. There is prayer in my house. A house of prayer means it is built on prayer. For Jesus to say that His house is to be called a house of prayer makes prayer essential to the people of God.

If a church is not focused on building prayer, then I don't know what they are building because they should not be building anything else. In my online prayer meetings, I tell my viewers, "If your church doesn't pray, you need to talk to your leader." Confront your leader and say, "I need to know what we are doing if we are not praying." Prayer is key.

At a women's retreat I held, I started by simply saying, "we are going to pray, and pray and pray and give room for the Holy Spirit to move." By the end of the weekend, I found medical alert bracelets on the altar. I asked if anyone left them by mistake. The response was that they no longer needed them, "We've been healed." A woman who attended had stroke symptoms, and the doctors couldn't figure out what was wrong. She said she felt knives in her head and was so disturbed by what was going on that her speech began to slur. She couldn't say, 'good morning.' Instead, she would say, 'morning good.' Her verbiage began to flip. The doctors could not determine what was going on, only that there was something neurologically wrong. She woke up the morning of the retreat unable to walk and had to use a cane. However, I have a video of her during the retreat, running around - completely healed! Completely healed. That weekend, God released that part of my ministry, and the healing services began, all because we prayed and made room for the Holy Spirit to move! From then on, we've launched several healing services. The first one was on November 12, 2022. It was a full-on healing crusade, open to anyone who wanted to come. We made room for the Holy Spirit. It is not about me. It is about the Holy Spirit doing His work because we believe in a God who heals. We believe in a God who delivers. We believe in a God who sets us free. You need to realize something about healing: we didn't come up with healing. We get this confused sometimes. We don't have to beg God to do what He said He would do. We don't have to convince God to heal. He is the one who told us about healing. So now, we just have to receive His Word and remind the devil he's defeated. Be a pursuer of what God promised you. Be that annoying widow who is knocking. Until when? Until your prayer is answered. Until your healing is received.

At that first healing service, a woman came that needed healing in her body. She came with her husband, but their marriage was falling apart and they were on the verge of a divorce. She was only coming for her body to be healed and never thought God would heal her marriage too. I began to preach and shared about the cross and the love of the Lord that sent Jesus to the cross. At that moment, she said in her heart, "Lord, could that love transform our marriage?" She looked at her husband and as they looked at each other, they felt like the Lord dropped new love in their hearts for each other. They began to weep and wept all the way home. They repented to each other and in her words, woke up to a new marriage! AND her body was also healed! God answers prayers!!

We need to live under an open heaven. An open heaven is a term that is frequently used in the church. What it means is that God's favor and blessing of God has opened up over our lives, and no blockages exist between God and us.But how many know that there are degrees in our relationship with God? There's blessed, and then there's abundantly blessed.

It is not that God has favorites. God wants all of us to live under an open heaven. It is His heart's desire to bless His people tremendously. But, often, there are people walking around feeling a disconnect between themselves and God. They want an open heaven without putting in the work. This open heaven concept can only be achieved through one word - obedience. Do you want to live under an open heaven? There is only one way and it is to live an obedient life. I can live in 90% obedience, but if there's still that 10% that's disobedient, it puts a cork in what God wants to do. We can say, *I love God*, but Jesus says we love Him when we obey Him. *Don't tell Me you love Me; obey Me. Don't tell Me you want to serve Me and walk in My ways; obey Me.* In other words, talk is cheap. God is saying to us that talk is cheap. *Obey Me.* I use the phrase 'reckless obedience' all the time and will continue to use it because it is how we've got to act. *Obey Me when you don't understand. Obey Me when it doesn't make sense. Obey Me when it seems foolish.* That is how an open heaven happens in the life of a believer; but unfortunately, I've found many believers that don't grab hold of this.

Maturity has nothing to do with longevity. It doesn't matter if you've been saved for 40 years and sat in the same seat every Sunday; that doesn't make you mature. You could be saved your whole life, but that doesn't make you mature. Maturity has nothing to do with longevity. Maturity has everything to do with honoring and walking in the Word of God. I have talked to people who have been saved their whole life and they can't understand forgiveness. I have to feed them spiritual milk. They've been saved for 40 years and they won't obey God. I know people who have been saved their whole life and don't tithe. Do you understand that if the Church, the members of all the churches actually tithed, the Church would lack nothing? Only 1.9% of the people who go to church tithe.

That's how low it is, 1.9%. People say, "Pastor, I can't pay my bills." I ask, "Do you tithe?" "Well, no," is what I hear in response. My answer is, "That's why you can't pay your bills." The Lord wants us to trust Him so that He can open the gates of heaven over us. Tithing is not because God needs our money. He doesn't need it. As a matter of fact, the entire 100% is His. God allows us to keep the 90%. That is the grace of God. He doesn't need our 10%. He owns the cattle upon a thousand hills. He could snap His fingers and do whatever He wants. The reason for tithing is to expose our obedience. God is not trying to get something *from* us; He is trying to get something *to* us. He uses our tithe as a seed of faith. It's a way to help us understand God's language so He can bless us. However, if we are not obedient, we are not ready for what He has for us, and He cannot release what He has to us. God won't open heaven if you don't want to walk in His rules. It is not that He doesn't love you or want to bless you or take care of you, but you will get significantly less if you don't trust and abide by his rules. He wants your trust to give you His best.

On one of my mission trips, a woman walked in off the streets after one of my services. She walked in with her face dropping, dragging her leg and arm. I said, "This woman's having a stroke. Why is she not going to the emergency room?" I was told that if she went to the emergency room, she would have to wait six hours and probably die there. She came for prayer. So we stopped and began to pray for her. And my prayer was like playing a game of handball. It hit the wall and came right back. That's when I knew something else was going on here. We began to talk and found that she was filled with unforgiveness. So we began to talk about forgiveness. She said, "I don't know anything about forgiveness." I asked, "Do you want to forgive?" She asked in return, "Is that what the Lord wants from me?" I said, "Yes, it is." She answered, "Will you help me? I don't know how to forgive." I said, "Forgiveness is a choice. It's not that you can't forgive but that you won't forgive." Family, we are all able to forgive but choose not to. It's a choice. After my explanation, she was willing and ready to forgive. I then walk her through prayers of forgiveness, and as we are praying, one right after the other, she forgives. I could feel it. She was loosed. I then prayed over her stroke, and instantly, her arm straightened up. Her face corrected itself, and she stood up. She began to walk normally, completely and totally healed.

Heaven opened over her as she began to forgive; that is what happened. Our good God desires that we would live under an open heaven, that there would be no blockage between Him and us. But there will always be a lack if there is unforgiveness in our life. God is looking for people who obey Him and obey Him, not 90%, not 95%, not 97%, but obey Him 100%. What you say God, I do.

Genesis 22 reads, "Now it came to pass after these things that God tested Abraham, and said to him, "Abraham!" And he said, "Here I am." Then He said, "Take now your son, your only son Isaac, whom you love, and go to the land of Moriah, and offer him there as a burnt offering on one of the mountains of which I shall tell you." So Abraham rose early in the morning and saddled his donkey, and took two of his young men with him, and Isaac his son; and he split the wood for the burnt offering, and arose and went to the place of which God had told him. Then on the third day Abraham lifted up his eyes and saw the place afar off. And Abraham said to the young men, "Stay here with the donkey; the lad and I will go yonder and worship, and we will come back to you." So Abraham took the wood of the burnt offering and laid it on Isaac, his son; and he took the fire in his hand, and a knife, and the two of them went together. But Isaac spoke to Abraham his father and said, "My father!" And he said, "Here I am, my son." Then he said, "Look, the fire and the wood, but where is the lamb for a burnt offering?" And Abraham said, "My son, God will provide for Himself the lamb for a burnt offering." So the two of them went together. Then they came to the place of which God had told him. And Abraham built an altar there and placed the wood in order; and he bound Isaac his son and laid him on the altar, upon the wood. And Abraham stretched out his hand and took the knife to slay his son. But the Angel of the Lord called to him from heaven and said, "Abraham, Abraham!" So he said, "Here I am." And he said, "Do not lay your hand on the lad, or do anything to him; for now I know that you fear God, since you have not withheld your son, your only son from Me." Then Abraham lifted his eyes and looked, and there behind him was a ram caught in the thicket by its horns. So Abraham went and took the ram, and offered it up for a burnt offering instead of his son. And Abraham called the name of the place, The-Lord-Will-Provide; as it is said to this day, "In the Mount of the Lord, it shall be provided." Then the Angel of the Lord called to Abraham a second time out of heaven, and said; "By Myself I have sworn, says the Lord, because you have done this thing, and have not withheld your son, your only son—blessing I will bless you, and multiplying I will multiply your descendants as the stars of the heaven and as the sand which is on the seashore; and your descendants shall possess the gate of their enemies. In your seed all the nations of the earth shall be blessed, because you have obeyed My voice."

Abraham received a promise from God that Isaac would be his seed and would bless the nations and all of his descendants would come from Isaac. But then God asked Abraham for the impossible: I want you to take your son, and I want you to offer him as a sacrifice to me.

The Bible says that Abraham takes the wood, takes everything he needs, takes his son, and walks for three days to the place God is showing him. Can you imagine what is going on in Abraham's mind while walking with his son? He sees the mountain ahead, and he hands Isaac the wood that he will sacrifice him on. As they are walking up, Isaac sees no offering and asks his father where it is. Abraham's response was, "God will provide." They get to the top, and he puts out the wood and binds his son. He binds him. What does that mean? He ties up his own son. Why? So that he wouldn't flinch or run. So he binds his son's hands and feet and puts him on the altar. Talk about reckless obedience. He lifts up the knife to kill his son and slices his throat.

And if you think he brought it up and said one Mississippi, two Mississippi, three Mississippi, that's not the case; there was no pause. This is what the book of Hebrews says to us about this. Hebrews 11:17-19, says, "By faith Abraham, when he was tested, offered up Isaac, and he who had received the promises offered up his only begotten son, of whom it was said, "In Isaac, your seed shall be called," concluding that God was able to raise him up, even from the dead, from which he also received him in a figurative sense." Abraham didn't lift up the knife and looked around, hoping for a solution. The Bible said that he knew that God would raise him from the dead. He raised up that knife intending to slit his son's throat, with confidence that God would raise him from the dead. That was his promise. I just have to obey. He lifts up the knife, and the Angel of the Lord stops him. The Angel of the Lord tells him not to harm the lad because God knows you love Him the most and is providing a ram for the sacrifice.

The Angel of the Lord then assures Abraham that because of his obedience, he will be blessed and his children will be blessed. His generations will be blessed, and his seed will be blessed. What is that called? It is called an open heaven. Heaven opened over Abraham at that moment because he loved God more. Our obedience says, 'I love you more. I trust you more.' Because of Abraham's obedience, there is still a Jewish nation to this day. God kept his promise to Abraham. How many nations have come for Israel? When you look at the map, Israel is surrounded on every side. And yet Israel stands. How many dictators tried to take Israel out? How many and how does God bless them? Have you ever heard the story of Oskar Schindler? He wasn't blessed until he guarded the Jews. Then, all of a sudden, everything in his life prospered. The day the war was over, everything in his life fell apart again because God blessed him for a moment to guard His people. Why? Because of this moment, one act of obedience blessed a generation. Heaven was open over them because of this man's obedience. Obedience opens heaven over your life. God is looking for a people, at this time, who knows how to obey God recklessly and not worry about the consequences. It is not your job to figure anything out. It is your job to obey. It is your job to do what God says. Let Him take care of the consequences. Let Him figure it out.

Abraham was convinced that God would raise Isaac from the dead. He knew God would work out the promise He gave him. As human beings, we think we must know all the details. We have to have all the information. A supernatural God doesn't have to explain Himself to us. We need to put things in perspective. A supernatural God doesn't have to explain Himself. God doesn't owe us an explanation. If He wants to give us one, great. And if He wants to tell us *what I say is none of your concern*, then He gets to say that too. That is maturity. Immaturity constantly asks why. *Why God? Why God? Why?* Maturity knows He's got this. All we need is our battle plan and our marching orders. I am a soldier, and I am going to obey My General. God is looking for people who understand how to obey Him by simply listening to what He says.

When we obey God, heaven opens. God looks at our obedience and sees faith; He sees our trust. If you struggle with anxiety in your life, it reveals a lack of trust. I love you enough to tell you the truth. Fear reveals a lack of faith because they are opposites. Anxiety reveals a lack of trust. Trust is like an onion. You don't ever fully trust something right away. You have to peel away at it. God, I trust You with my finances, my children, my health, and my future. God begins to peel away these layers. We need to begin to trust God in one area at a time until all the layers are peeled away. Anxiety reveals a part of your heart that doesn't fully trust the Lord. And that's okay.

Now let's mature. It's okay when something gets exposed; now mature in it. That is what maturity looks like. I've had so many believers say, "Pastor, this is just how I am." No, that is how you accept being. It's not how you are; it's what you have accepted. The Word of God is sufficient. So if you are struggling with something, you don't have to stay there; you just have to decide to mature. Ask, *Lord, what has to grow in me?* But if you say, *Lord, I don't obey you, or I don't obey you 100%, God. I have to figure it all out before I obey you. And if I don't like it, I'm going to hesitate.* If that is what you do, you will live without the full blessing of God. You'll make it to heaven, but you won't live the way God wants you to live on planet Earth. Two-thirds of believers will never fulfill God's calling on their life here on Earth. Two-thirds will never walk in the fullness God has for them. They will make it to heaven but would have lived short here. Why? Because they won't obey him recklessly. Why? Because they have to have it on their terms, it has to be their way. To recklessly obey God means it is not about our terms but about His terms and what He says.

A huge part of recklessly obeying God is learning to walk humbly. What does that mean? It means that I don't always have to be in the right. I can be wrong and humble myself before the Lord. When I graduated from Bible school, I was offered many positions. But God said 'No' to all of them. All of them. Where does God put me? He put me in a church that did not recognize females in ministry. The Lord said, "I want you to serve there." So I did. And there was one particular day that I was working and doing what I needed to do. I was cleaning the classroom. And I remember having a temper tantrum with God. Now you have to throw some grace towards me; I was only 22 at the time. Picture this, I am in the classroom, mad and sweeping the floor; I am angry. All the prophetic words, all the teachings in my life for me to be doing this? I was waiting for Jesus to comfort me, but that's not what happened. I heard the Lord say, "And so what if it is? What if all this time, the words, and the training were for you to sweep this floor for Me? Would you not do it for My glory?" And I said, "Lord, I will stand here and sweep this floor every day if it brings You glory." And that was it. All my anger left.

I continued to work at that church for a little longer. One day, I attended an event, and a senior pastor at another church saw me. God spoke to him ,and he hired me to be his youth pastor. God proved Himself faithful in the growth of that youth ministry. One moment created another moment. If I didn't respond to God humbly, willing to sweep the floor for His glory, the other moment would never have happened. That step of obedience created the open door. That is how heaven opens. Heaven opens as we walk in obedience. God opens heaven in front of us; doors open out of obedience. But something else can also happen. Sometimes a door is shut because God is protecting you. God is looking for people like Abraham. Abraham didn't understand why God wanted him to kill his son, the son God promised him. He thought God would resurrect Isaac from the dead, so he obeyed God. God is looking for people that obey him recklessly. God shows up when we say, *God, whatever You say, my answer is yes. Whatever the cost, my answer is yes.* God shows up in that. We must understand that as mature as we are and as old as we are, we are still His children. And we need to operate like that. Whatever our Father says, we do.

We need to understand our role as the Church. Obedience is the difference between the people of God who are Remnants and those who are just playing church. The difference is obedience. If God wants us to love our enemies, we'll love our enemies. If He wants us to bless those persecuting us, We must do it. You do it because He told you to do it. If God tells you to love someone that is miserable towards you, you love them because He told you to. You buy a cup of coffee for your boss who's nasty to you all the time, because God told you to do it. We all want to obey when it is easy. It's easy to love that wonderful neighbor, but what happens when He tells you to love the nasty one? God wants us to obey Him without limits.

All we need to understand is that we don't know better than God. And when God asks you to obey, if you want your life blessed, you obey. You obey whatever He says. One day, I went to a doctor's appointment, and God said, "I want you to go to the cafeteria." I responded, "I don't want anything from the cafeteria." He repeated, "Go to the cafeteria." So I went to the cafeteria. I'm just obeying God. He said, "Get in line for a cup of tea." I didn't want a cup of tea, but I got in line for a cup of tea. As I'm standing in line, the woman in front of me has my video on her phone. She's watching my devotion. So I tap her on the shoulder. She turned, wondering what was happening. I said, "You're watching my video."

I don't know this woman but she said the video inspired her. I said, "Can I tell you why you're inspired?" And in the middle of the cafeteria, I shared the Lord Jesus Christ with her. Obedience led to a new soul. Heaven opened. We need to learn to live in 100% reckless obedience to the Lord at all costs, and when you do, your life will dramatically shift. There will be blessing upon blessing and doors upon doors will open. God is looking for people who will obey Him recklessly, 100% of the time. Not 97%, not 98%, not 99%. *What You say, I'll do.* We need to begin to declare that before God. Tell God you will obey Him, and then God will test you. He'll throw something your way. And if you want to grow in God, obey quickly.

Then you'll be more sensitive to His voice and obey quicker. As you do that, you will feel like everything seems blessed. Obedience speaks to God of love and speaks to God of faith. God looks at that and says, *Okay, I can now bless them more. I can give them more because they trust Me. They trust Me.* Do you want to tell God you trust Him? Don't say it. Do it. Do you want to tell God you love Him? Don't say it. Do it. Do you want to tell God you believe what He says? Don't say it, do it. Don't worry about the results. If He tells you to pray for someone, just pray for them. You might say, *Well, Lord, they didn't get healed.* You are not the healer. It's not your business. And planning is not your business either. Your business is doing what God's asking you to do. He is in charge of the results; you are responsible for your obedience. Heaven opens, Child of God. Heaven opens.

SUPERNATURAL

St. Francis of Assisi said, "Preach the gospel at all times, and if necessary, use words." Your life is the Gospel. How you live is the Gospel. It is not what you call yourself. It is not the pretty cross on your neck. What does your life say? God is raising up, in this time, a Remnant people to combat what is in front of us. Isaiah 59:19 says, "When the enemy comes in like a flood, the Spirit of the Lord will lift up a standard against him." If we look back in the Word, we find that God has always raised up a people to fight the darkness. That has been the standard; God has raised up people when the enemy has come in full force, just like now. 1 Peter states that in the last days, the enemy will stand in plain sight, bold and bracing and nobody will see him. That is what is happening right now. We are seeing the words in 1 Peter become a reality right before our eyes.

But God has always raised up a people. When there was a Goliath, there was a David. When there was a Pharaoh, there was a Moses. When there was Jericho, there was a Joshua. When there was a Nebuchadnezzar, there was a Daniel. When there was a Hitler, there was Dietrich Bonhoeffer. When there was a Karl Marx, there was a Charles Spurgeon. And right now, with this anti-Christ demonic agenda, make no doubt about it; what we are looking at is not of man. It is demonic. It is straight from the pit of hell. We see this anti-Christ agenda filling our streets and filling our schools. They are giving 10-year-olds hormone-blocking medicine and allowing them to cut off their genitalia. You cannot tell me that is not demonic.

That is demonic and from the pit of hell. They can't consent to sex, but they can consent to that? This anti-Christ spirit wants to fill our streets, fill our schools, fill our government, and, if possible, fill our churches. God's response to this is to raise up people on fire with His Spirit, who understand who they are and who they serve. God is raising up a Remnant people that will live and move in power, in His power, to be who they are supposed to be. People who will remain. That is God's response. The Remnant are consistent and they don't move. They know who they are and they know who they serve. They have surrendered to Him and they stand their ground. They are a Remnant people. They are not moved by culture. Culture doesn't shift them. TikTok doesn't shift them. The government doesn't shift them. Instagram doesn't shift them. How many 'likes' they have doesn't shift them and they don't care how many people may hate them.

We need to stop caring about what people think. What cured Charles Spurgeon of the fear of man was the fear of God. The Remnant people fear God. If everyone turns their back on us, we are in good company because they first did it to Jesus. *Pastor, they are going to get offended.* The Bible says the Gospel is an offense. The Scriptures are an offense. I'd rather you be offended. Even hate me, if you'll surrender. What I won't do is just be quiet and watch you burn. That's the truth of the Gospel. Remnant people stand their ground; they know where they stand. God is raising a Remnant people for one main reason; King Jesus is coming. Do you feel that in your bones? King Jesus is coming, and the

Remnant people must get their house in order before His return. They understand that they are supernatural.

They are a people who understand they are a people of the Spirit. They understand that they are a people that live and dwell in the Spirit. I am in this world, but I am not of this world. It means that I am physically in this world, but my DNA is not from this world. I was bought with Someone's blood, so my DNA now belongs to heaven. My DNA is Kingdom-bound. I am in this world, but I am a citizen of heaven. So when people start talking about recession, don't let it concern you because your citizenship is elsewhere. There is no recession in heaven. Let the banks freeze. Our God owns the cattle on a thousand hills. We are in this world but not of this world. Our citizenship is elsewhere. We started a supernatural journey the day we gave our life to Jesus.

That is why the Bible calls it 'born again.' You were dead in your transgressions and sin. You had no Spirit or life, period. You were dead. But when you gave your life to Jesus, your spirit was born. That day, you started a spiritual journey; you started a spiritual life. It was not meant to be a once-in-a-lifetime occurrence. It was meant to be how you walk from now on. You are in the Spirit, a supernatural being, born of God, and the Spirit of God dwells in you. Do you understand that everywhere you go, the Spirit of God goes too? You walk and the Gospel walks with you; the Spirit of God is there. You walk into Longhorn, the Spirit of God is there. You go to the gas station, the Spirit of God is there. If you consider yourself a Child of God, the Spirit of God should be the greatest voice in your life. The Spirit of God should be the greatest component of your life. Everything else is subservient to it. However, that is not how we have been living. We live in our flesh, and then, when we are in trouble, we try to tap into the Spirit of God. How sad for us. God said, "I've come to give you life and life more abundantly."

God came to give us this abundant life; however, we cannot have life more abundantly unless we walk in the Spirit. Galatians 5:16, tells us, "Walk in the Spirit, and you shall not fulfill the lust of the flesh." That is the solution to overcoming sin. *But Pastor, I can't overcome sin.* I then respond, "Do you walk in the Spirit?" That's the answer. God has made it so simple, but we are the ones who complicate it. Walk in the Spirit, and you will not fulfill the lust of the flesh. Walk with Him in the Spirit, and you won't fulfill the lust of the flesh. We must walk in the Spirit and understand that the Remnant people are supernatural beings. There is a clear marker in the early Church that is missing in today's church: that marker is faith. Until now, we've been very creative in thinking we didn't need it. However, the Bible is clear that without faith, you cannot please God. So if you're trying to please God and don't have faith, you are failing. You cannot please God without faith; it is impossible.

It is impossible to please God without faith because anyone that comes must believe that He is a rewarder of those that diligently seek Him. If you don't have faith, you cannot please God. Faith is the currency of heaven. Faith is the language that God hears. If you want the Holy Spirit to be active and supernatural in your life, the activating agent is faith. It is the key ingredient. Faith is the key ingredient to walking in the Spirit.

When you operate in faith, you allow the Spirit of God to lead you. In return, you automatically get all His blessings. When you obey the Spirit of God, that act of faith releases heaven over your life. If you want to understand why you may not see the results you seek, take a moment and reflect on your faith. When you trust God, faith is released. When you hold back in your flesh, you hold back the Hands of God. God is looking to infuse his people with faith.

Matthew 14, starting with verse 22, says, "Immediately Jesus made His disciples get into the boat and go before Him to the other side, while He sent the multitudes away. And when He had sent the multitudes away, He went up on the mountain by Himself to pray. Now when evening came, He was alone there. But the boat was now in the middle of the sea, tossed by the waves, for the wind was contrary. Now in the fourth watch of the night Jesus went to them, walking on the sea. And when the disciples saw him walking on the sea, they were troubled, saying, "It is a ghost!" And they cried out for fear. But immediately Jesus spoke to them, saying, "Be of good cheer! It is I; do not be afraid." And Peter answered Him and said, "Lord, if it is You, command me to come to You on the water." So He said, "Come." And when Peter had come down out of the boat, he walked on the water to go to Jesus. But when he saw that the wind was boisterous, he was afraid; and beginning to sink he cried out, saying, "Lord, save me!" And immediately Jesus stretched out His hand and caught him, and said to him, "O you of little faith, why did you doubt?" And when they got into the boat, the wind ceased. Then those who were in the boat came and worshiped Him saying, "Truly You are the Son of God."

Let's look at this story further. Jesus has just fed the 5,000. He immediately sends the disciples to go by boat to the other side while He goes to pray. The disciples are in the water, and they hit a storm. They are struggling in this storm. These are seasoned fishermen; storms are their business. When you have a storm that scares the fishermen, that is a pretty big storm. They are scared. They are bouncing around in this boat and cannot move an inch either way. The storm pushes them back every time. It is a massive storm that they cannot overcome.

In the middle of the storm, they look and see what appears to be a ghost walking on water. Can you imagine? It's the middle of the night, and this creature is walking on water toward them. They are afraid. Jesus yells to them and says, "Don't be afraid; it is I. It is me." And Peter stands up and says, "Lord, if it's you, command me to come to You on the water." And Jesus immediately says, "Come." Peter walks out on the water towards Jesus. He then comes to a certain point, looks down at the waves and sinks. Fearful, he asks Jesus to save him. Jesus immediately stretches out His hand and pulls him back up, saying, "O you of little faith, why did you doubt?" He walks him back into the boat and then the storm stops.

There are a few things we need to understand in this story. First, it is a storm that all their skills and experience could not help them with. Everything they knew in the flesh could not help them. They could not defeat it, and they were in trouble. Jesus, because He is Jesus, came walking on the very waves that they couldn't defeat. He defeated them with his feet. They were caught in a storm that their boat could not navigate over, but Jesus strolled on those very waves. He walked…in a storm…on the same water their boat could not navigate through…because He is Jesus. But then Peter saw Him, realized who He was, and asked the Lord to command him to come to Him.

Did the storm stop when Peter asked that? No, the storm did not stop. The storm was still as active as it was before. What changed? Peter changed. Peter's perspective changed because Jesus became much bigger than the storm he was in. The presence of Jesus altered what he was walking through, and he began to activate his faith. He had lost his faith because of the storm, but when he saw the size of his Lord, he wanted to walk on water. Peter did exactly what Jesus did. He began to walk on the same water he couldn't get his boat over; Peter was now walking on it with his feet. Why? Because of where he was looking. The wind was still blowing and everything was still dangerous. But Peter had changed. Peter had activated his faith, and now he is walking. Then he remembered the storm, and he began to sink. He took his eyes off Jesus, and he began to sink. He cried, "Lord, save me," and the Lord pulled him up.

Does Jesus comfort him? No. Instead of comforting him, Jesus asks Peter why he had such little faith. Jesus gave him a nice little kick. He wanted to know why Peter was afraid. After all, He was right next to him. He was right there. How could he have such little faith?

The Lord says to us today, *what are you afraid of? I am right here. I am with you; I am for you. What are you afraid of? Where is your faith, Child of God?* Peter began to understand that the key to activating his faith was actually getting out of the boat. As long as you, Child of God, are in the boat, you are not activating your faith; you are trusting in everything that you know. But the minute you step out of the boat, that is when you have activated your faith. And it was right there when Peter began his journey to understand what faith was supposed to look like. A clear picture of faith is simple: I am looking at God, and my God is bigger than the storm in front of me. Faith is the substance of things hoped for, the evidence of things not seen. It is a substance.

Faith is tangible. It is tangible because I can look at a Holy God, I can read His Word, I can know who He is, and I can stand on it. Faith is not allowing the storm to be bigger than my God. The storm didn't go away; Peter just had victory over it. We've walked through Covid for many years now. I don't ever deny what Covid is. I have done more funerals than I've wanted to because of Covid. What I will deny is its authority over me. There is a big difference. I don't have to deny the storm, I just have to deny its authority. I don't deny the storm. The storm is real, but my God is more real. That's the difference. That's what faith is. It does not deny the doctor's reports; it's saying God is Lord over it. That's the difference faith makes. It's not coming under the storm; it's rising above it.

John G. Lake was a missionary from America who went to Africa in 1906. It took him two months to get to Africa by boat. He went there because the Holy Spirit told him to take his family and go. He didn't know where in Africa he was going. Nevertheless, he sold everything and traveled to Africa with his wife and five children. The part he was certain of was that he had to obey God. He arrived in the middle of South Africa and stood on the dock with his wife and children. God had specifically instructed him to wait on the dock. Four hours later, a woman came up to him and asked if he was the missionary from America. He tells her he is. She tells him that the Lord instructed her to give him her house. So she picks them up and takes them to the house.

John G. Lake had arrived amid a pandemic. People were dying in the streets with no one to bury them. The pandemic had gripped the people with the fear of being contaminated with the virus, which meant nobody would go near the dead. So his first job there was to bury the dead. That became his job. He began to bury the people in the street, and the people wouldn't go near him. They couldn't believe he wasn't afraid. To demonstrate this even further, he put his hand inside the mouth of a dead person and put saliva on his hand. John understood that the saliva had the law of death in it, but he knew he was a child of the most high God, so he had the law of life in him, which meant the virus died in his hand. John G. Lake then started healing schools all over Africa, where millions(not thousands) were healed. They received healing because he understood who he was and Who he served.

In 2020, satan released a spirit of sickness on our world. Satan released it; keep that in mind. God didn't release it; Satan did. He is the law of death. But more than the spirit of sickness, what was released was the spirit of fear. Fear is greater than the spirit of sickness. We must stop treating fear like it is just an emotion; it's not an emotion. The Bible calls it a spirit. He has not given you a spirit of fear but of power and love and a sound mind. It is a spirit. And how do you deal with a spirit? You rebuke it. You don't ignore it. You don't hope it goes away, you rebuke it, and you treat it like a spirit. Fear infested people's lives, and it has infested the Church. As we read in Isaiah 59, when the enemy came in like a flood, God raised up something. What is the response to the spirit of fear? It's a Church filled with faith because the opposite of fear is faith. God is looking for a people He can fill with faith and who understand what it is to be the Church on a mission. A people ready to do their job at this hour and in this time.

That's who we ought to be. It'll never happen if I don't step out. People will not know if we don't do our job. We need to get out of the boat. Every one of our boats looks different, but we all need to open up our mouths. You need to begin to be His voice and be His people. Don't worry about making a mistake. Make a mistake for goodness sake. Better to do something in faith than nothing in fear. God is looking for people willing to walk on water and not be afraid. Fear has come in to grip us and we need to, as the people of God, brush it off and become fearless. The time and the hour we live in call for us to step out.

As I've mentioned before, I travel a great deal but my home church is in Staten Island, New York. On Christmas of 2021, my pastor's wife, Emma, fell ill with Covid. Initially, it wasn't a big deal, and she would complain of being bored at home. We would talk or text all the time. One day, Emma was a little tired and I told her to rest. Then the next day, her back was a little tight. All this time, we are praying. The next day, I get a text from the pastor; he is rushing her to the hospital. She had double pneumonia. They seemed to have caught the pneumonia early enough and began treatment with oxygen and antibiotics. Within 24 hours, she couldn't breathe and needed a ventilator so her lungs could rest. They planned to remove the vent in a few days, and she would then be fine. By the third day, the doctor called the pastor and told him that she had every complication that could come from Covid.

Her kidneys were not functioning. She needed 100% oxygen and was unresponsive. The doctor told the pastor that she would not make it through the night and that he should get her papers in order. Pastor then reached out to all of us. The storm is high. It doesn't get much higher than that. We called the Church. We called everyone together and we just began to declare the Word of God. Fifty church members stood outside the hospital on the coldest day in December and began to declare the Word of God. Security came out to see what was going on and left them alone. They were warring for hours. They saw the storm, but they also saw their God. I went on her Facebook page because I wanted a picture of her to shoot out to my prayer group for prayer but what I found was the last verse she posted. It was from 2 Chronicles 20:17, *Stand firm and wait to see My deliverance today.*

I pulled it out and posted it. I said on the post, *Emma, from your mouth, we are going to prophesy.* I asked the Church to pray this verse. I also asked them if they would call her by name when they prayed. Say, *Emma, get up in the Name of Jesus. Emma, arise from your sick bed.* Jesus used names. *Lazarus, come forth. Zacchaeus, come out of the tree.* Call Emma by name. Together we began to pray and to declare. We saw the storm, but our God was bigger. In 24 hours, everything shifted. Her kidneys, which had completely failed, were now functioning independently. Her oxygen came up to full breath. Within a week or so, she was off the vent. She preached at the church on Mother's Day of the same year. I asked her if she remembered anything when she was on the vent. She answered, "I remember being intubated, and I remember them pulling it out. The only memory I have is of people calling my name. Emma. Emma. Like they were trying to wake me up. That's all I remember is people calling my name."

Don't tell me my God does not do the miraculous. Don't tell me my God is not able. He is more than able. He is more than willing. He is looking for a people that will stand in faith, declare His Word, stand in their authority, and be the Church.

God is looking for people willing to get out of the boat. At this time, in this season, when the enemy's rising up like a flood, God is looking for a people who are willing to be the standard. He's looking for a people who are going to say, *God, I don't have the tools, but if you equip me, I'll do it. I'm willing to stand. I'm willing to be the Church because the enemy will not have a victory on my watch. The enemy is not going to take our children on my watch. He is not going to wreck the church on my watch. I'm present, and the Spirit of God is in me. And I am a supernatural being.* The supernatural should be in our daily life. Every day, you should be experiencing the supernatural. If you aren't experiencing this every day, you need to up your game and say, *God, open up the supernatural in my life. I want You to move through me because I believe that You can.*

Pray with me!

God, we bless you. Worthy is the lamb of God. Worthy are You, King Jesus. We give You praise. You alone are worthy. We don't care that the wind blows, God. Let it blow. Let the storms rise. You are greater, God. You are more mighty, God. Let the enemy bring his best; You are greater. You already defeated him. Satan, let us remind you that Jesus already defeated you. We don't fight for victory; we fight from victory. We're not afraid of the terror that comes by night. A thousand will fall, ten thousand at our right hand and it will not harm us.

God, I want You to infuse us with faith. (PRAY THIS OUT LOUD) I want to be able to get out of the boat, God. I am not going to stay in the boat and be comfortable. I want to get out of the boat, but I need the courage. I need faith, God. I want faith. I want to increase the faith in my life today. I want to increase my faith today. Amen.

An Unshakeable People

I live by this motto: The "yes" is my business; everything else is God's business. I've already mentioned this many times throughout this book, and I've done it intentionally. I want to instill this in you. My obedience is my business, and everything else is God's business. God was so faithful when I built a revival ministry amid a pandemic. God used it to bring many people to Him. We have witnessed healing, freedom, and connections. It's ridiculous to think that you could bear fruit in the middle of something fruitless, but God did just that.

At one of our healing services, a woman came who hadn't left her house in 5 years! She was very sick and struggled to move. Barely any visitors came. She was sick, lonely, in pain, discouraged, and saw no end in sight. She prayed with us regularly online and heard about the healing service. She felt the Lord told her to go but questioned how. She needed a special van to take her; she needed support to walk and had not been around people in years because she struggled with crowds. However, she knew God was speaking to her, and she said yes. She rented a special van, reached out to some friends to support her, and reserved equipment to help her walk. She had to get a driver and traveled over an hour to the service. She was excited and nervous at the same time. She entered the church and just stood in the lobby. I happened to be in the lobby at the same time. I saw her, walked over and welcomed her by name. I asked if I could hug her and she started to cry and said yes, please. I gave her a gentle hug, and her healing started then. She entered the service using a walker and left walking the walker! Her words were, "I just wanted to obey the Lord and did not know what to expect after that." Her whole being was healed- mind, body, soul, and emotions. The yes is our business; everything else is Gods!

I've worked in many churches and have served on many platforms, but I've never been more excited about being a Christian more than now. I know I've expressed this before, but it's true. You might say, "Is she for real? Does she see what's going on?" Oh, yes, I see it. And I get excited that God would give me the privilege of being alive at this moment, in time. Think about it. He could have picked anybody. Moses could be alive right now. Joshua could be alive right now, but He chose us to be alive right now. He chose us. So if He chose us, He's called us.

If we are breathing on this planet at this moment and we call ourselves the Church, then God is in it. The year 2020 was like a bad dream in some sense. It seemed like the plot thickened and got worse every day. Unfortunately, we saw a lot of confusion and my heart broke because of it. I had no idea why the Church was confused. The world should have been confused. It had every right to be confused but the Church should have become laser-sharp.

The Church should have realized that Jesus is coming and God is preparing us for His return. The Church should have been laser-sharp. Part of the deception is that we needed something more than the cross. We needed something more than Jesus. We needed something more than His blood and His resurrection. But I can say with full confidence that the cross has always been more than enough. The cross is sufficient. It is Jesus plus nothing equals everything. That is the formula. He is more than enough.

God is raising up a people. He is forming an army. You might look at yourself and say *I am not equipped.* In the Old Testament, King Jehoshaphat was surrounded by armies, and he prayed, "God, we are outnumbered on every end. We are outnumbered, God. We have no recourse against this vast army coming at us, but our eyes are on you." And God answered Jehoshaphat; "You are not going to have to fight. Just go to your position. I will do the work."

The problem is that we are not living as Remnant people; we are not using the correct strategy to fight. We must learn to live offensively and not defensively. We are playing this game the wrong way. We are sitting around waiting for the next attack. But we don't realize, Church, that we are the attack. The Church of Jesus Christ is the attack. Do you understand why God hasn't judged America? Because the Remnant is here. Abraham made a plea for Sodom and Gomorrah. He asked God if there were 50, would He spare them? Then it was 40, 30, 20 all the way to 10 and God said, "yes." God is looking and saying; *I can't judge America. My people are there.* Why do you think the rapture is so significant? The reason that America has hope is because the Church is present. The hope of the world is the Church of Jesus Christ.

Our offensive game should look like that of King David facing Goliath. David was basically saying *I'm not afraid of Goliath, Goliath should be afraid of me. Does he know who my Father is?* God is looking for unshakeable people, and I believe God is raising us

151

up to be unshakeable. People tell me that they see things shifting daily: the stock market, gas prices, jobs, and banking. Every day they see something else is shifting and they want to know when it will stop.

The answer is very simple. It is going to stop when we become unshakeable. Everything will keep shifting until we become unshakeable. God is raising up a people that are going to be unshakeable. Their dependency is going to be in the Lord. Their hope is going to be in the Lord. Their faith is going to be in the Lord. Their provision is going to be from the Lord. The stock market is not going to feed them. God will send ravens to feed them. It will not be through their bank accounts because their Father owns the cattle on a thousand hills. Their hope will not be in doctors or the medical system. We have Dr. Jesus; we're all good. God is raising up a people who walk and live depending solely on Him; after everything has been shaken in them, they still stand. Like a siphon drains and pulls everything out, God wants only what honors Him left. Why? Because God is looking for people that are Jesus and Jesus only. People that are not holding anything dearer than they are holding King Jesus. God is raising us up in this hour to stand and stand for Him. To be a light in the midst of the darkness.

During the riots in 2020, I posted something on social media and received both positive and negative feedback. One particular person commented and explained how they felt my posts were a little too strong because there were a lot of people hurting during a very dark time. I then asked a very simple question. "When do people need a flashlight? When it's dark or when everyone can see?" When it's dark, you need light to show the way and the job of the Church, and the job of leaders in the Church is to act like a flashlight saying, "You are all going the wrong way. This is the way to walk. This is the way to live." That is the job of the Church. We are the hope of the world. You need to understand that in every place you put your foot, the kingdom should advance. When you walk into Costco, the kingdom should walk in with you. When you go get gas, the kingdom should walk in with you. Everywhere you go, the kingdom should advance with you, and I believe God is doing just that. He is raising up a people that are going to be fearless, courageous and will stand in this hour and say, "This is the way, this is the way."

Take the word revival. You've probably heard it so many times in this book. God has called me to be a "revivalist." I did a lot of research on what that means. The word "revival" is so simple in its definition. It means to go back to your origin; go back to the beginning. Revival is to go back to how this all started because the Church that Jesus started was unshakeable.

Acts 3:1 reads, "Now Peter and John went up together to the temple at the hour of prayer, in the ninth hour. And a certain man lame from his mother's womb was carried, whom they laid daily at the gate of the temple which is called Beautiful, to ask alms from those who entered the temple; who, seeing Peter and John about to go into the temple, asked for alms. And fixing his eyes on him, with John, Peter said, "Look at us." So he gave them his attention, expecting to receive something from them. Then Peter said, "Silver and gold I do not have, but what I do have I give you: In the name of Jesus Christ of Nazareth, rise up and walk." And he took him by the right hand and lifted him up, and immediately his feet and ankle bones received strength. So he, leaping up, stood and walked and entered the temple with them - walking, leaping and praising God. And all the people saw him walking and praising God. Then they knew that it was he who sat begging alms at the Beautiful Gate of the temple; and they were filled with wonder and amazement at what had happened to him."

I mentioned this story early, but let's dive deeper and unpack it together. Peter and John are filled with the Spirit of God. They are going about their daily life. They are on their way to pray as they always do. As they come to the temple, they find a man that has been lame his whole life, and this man sees them and asks them for money. Peter then gives him an instruction and tells him to look at them. Peter says to him, "Silver and gold I do not have, but what I do have I give you: In the name of Jesus Christ of Nazareth, rise up and walk." As Peter gives the lame man this instruction, he simultaneously grabs the man's hand to lift him up. There is no pause between the instruction and the action. It's almost in one movement. He pulls him up; the man gains strength in his legs and begins jumping, leaping, and walking. He walks into the temple. Everyone is astonished.

Peter and John were aware that there would be backlash from this miracle. They knew very well who they were dealing with. They saw the Pharisees attack Jesus, and they saw how they followed Jesus. They knew, and they didn't care. They saw a man who needed to be healed and were willing to stand. Later, the Bible tells us they would be arrested and told not to preach. But Peter and John stood their ground. There was no way they would stop preaching. They were going to continue to preach in the Name of Jesus.

What Peter said to that man was so important. I want to concentrate on what Peter says to him because it's so important. "Silver and gold I do not have, but what I do have I give you: In the name of Jesus." What did Peter have? "What I have, I give you." He had the power and the anointing of the Spirit of God. He had the faith that overcomes this world.

Peter had no problem saying, "What I do have, I give you." Because he knew that he had it. He knew the Lord was with him, the anointing was on him, and he could hear God. He was abiding in the Lord, and he had the presence of the Spirit of God. God is raising up a people that would do exactly the same thing. I have this to offer you.

1 John 5:4, says, "For whatever is born of God overcomes the world." The victory that overcomes the world - is our faith. Our faith is what makes us unshakable. Our faith is tangible. It is tangible evidence to us of the power of the Living God. And through the power of the Living God, He is making a people so incredibly increased in faith. So much so that we are not going to need doctors. We are going to know how to lay hands on the sick. We will have the faith to pray and believe God to show up. We are going to pray and watch our prodigals come home. We are not going to allow what we see to diminish our faith. Faith is the substance of things not seen. Faith doesn't go by what I see; it goes by what I know.

Don't concern yourselves with the silver and the gold. Have the Spirit of God be overwhelming in your faith; be overwhelming in the presence of the Lord; be overwhelming in the infilling of the Spirit of God. Don't worry about what you don't have. Have the Holy Spirit. Silver and gold I don't have, but what I do have, I give you.

During one of my mission trips to Mexico, we visited a boy's home. This boys' home consisted of about 20 boys; all were what they called street boys. They were either found wandering the streets and living on their own or they were removed from their home for one reason or another. Many don't have parents, or if they do, their parents cannot care for them. Some of the boys were used for drugs or even sold for sex for the parents to acquire money. They are very broken and hurt boys. I took the team there for the day to minister to these boys. We brought food, balls, and games with us. We taught them worship songs and did some skits for them about Jesus. While we were there, one team member noticed a really little boy in the corner. Most of the boys were older (most don't even know their age, so we had to assume), but this little boy looked about six years old. The team member went to talk with him and he just began to cry. He explained that he had only been there a week and had no idea why he was there, and he was so lonely. We spoke to the people in charge, and they said that he was removed from his house because his parents were drug users and he was found basically starving and without any care. He was so little that he simply just wanted his mom. Our hearts broke for him as he repeatedly said I don't have anyone to hug me. We prayed with him and shared the Lord with him, and he was better but still yearning for a hug from his mom. The team member who first noticed him said that she felt that if he could have a teddy bear to hold, it would give him so much peace. I thought it was a wonderful idea, but we are nowhere near any toy store. As a matter of fact, we are in a deserted part of town with just a little corner store for milk and basic toiletries. However, she was sure of what she felt, so we prayed together and decided to pick up ice cream for the boys from a store nearby.

As we are walking, I see this little hole-in-the-wall store; the whole outside is broken. We walk inside and there is nothing in the store but a display case. It is completely empty, except for one item, a teddy bear!! We began to scream; we could not believe what we were seeing. I ask the owner how much for the teddy bear, he says "five dollars." We laugh, give five dollars and run back to the house. As we hand the little boy the teddy bear, he starts to cry and says, "now I have someone to hug every night." We tell him that Jesus gave him the bear, and his smile fills the room. Silver and gold we did not have, but what we had was enough!

What I have is sufficient. What you have today is sufficient. If the Spirit of God dwells in you, Child of God, it is sufficient for what is coming your way. All you have to do is walk in it. The Bible says, "signs and wonders follow," it is a motion; it is a verb. I am not sitting. Sometimes we wait for the Spirit of God to kick us; He already told us to go. He is not going to say it again. God is saying, *Go, be My Church. Go, be My people, speak for Me. Be My ambassadors in this dark hour, and speak the truth.* I am a proud immigrant from the Middle East, and I am a proud American. I love this country, but this country needs revival.

Our country is in danger, and we need to stand. Charles Spurgeon preached Karl Marx and his ungodly theology right out of his country by telling the truth, and we need to do the same. He stood at his podium and said, "Not on my watch, not while there's breath in my lungs. Not while the Spirit of God is alive and well. I will stand and do my job in this hour."

God is raising up a people today with the same spirit as Spurgeon saying, *Not on my watch. You will not take this country. You will not take our young people. We stand in our spot and say not today.* We will do our job because what we have is sufficient. The Spirit of God is in us. We just need to activate it by walking. We need to activate it by obeying. We serve a God that can do anything. Once you understand the size of our God, you will fight differently.

I believe we will begin to step into some supernatural things like we've never seen, and God is looking for people who understand that what overcomes the world is their faith in Him. As mentioned before, prior to becoming a revivalist, I was the family life pastor and ran the Vacation Bible School there. One year I decided to move the same week as the Vacation Bible School because why not?

On the last day of VBS, I had a young girl staying with me who was interning. I ran out of my house to go to Vacation Bible School. I locked the garage and then realized that I didn't have the key and had locked myself out. I didn't have time then to deal with it at that moment; I had to get to work. I told myself that I would deal with this when I returned home after finishing VBS. I get home at one thirty in the morning and I go to the garage and it is then that I remember I do not have the key. I go to the front door and the screen door is locked. I don't have that key either. So the young girl with me says, "Don't worry, pastor. I'm going to check the windows. Maybe there's a window open." I'm like, "Girl, don't waste your time. I'm from Brooklyn. Those windows are deadbolted. They are not open. A mosquito couldn't get in my house."

"What do we do?" she said. And I replied, "You know what? I'll break the door." So I put all my force on the handle and hoped to break the door, and then I realized that the handle is just decoration. It's a deadbolt. At this point, I was exhausted. I lifted my hands before the Lord and said, "Lord, I need you. Lord, I need you." As God is my witness, as we were both looking at the lock through the glass from the other side, I saw the lock begin to turn! It just began to turn and we're watching and watching, and then we hear a click and the door opens. She looked at me and I looked at her. "Um, Pastor?" she said. I said, "Yep. Did an angel unlock the door?" she asks, "I think so." I said. "What do we do?" she asked. I said, "We open the door." So I put my hand on the handle and began to pull the door that before was completely locked, and was now completely open. I opened the door and when the door passed me, I heard the Holy Spirit say, "There is no door I cannot open; there is no door I cannot open." God is telling us that when He wants to open a door for His children, there is no chain, or deadbolt, or anything else that will stop Him. Nothing will stand in His way when He wants to make a way for His children, nothing.

You don't have to shake, Child of God. You can be unshakeable because our God can open any door. Nothing stops the Hand of your God. Your God is big, mighty and strong. He's equipped you for this hour. He's equipped you for this moment. Don't be afraid. Rebuke that spirit of fear. The Bible calls it a spirit. Rebuke it; don't entertain it. Rebuke that spirit of anxiety. We break down depression today in the Name of Jesus. You foul spirit, we break your lying mouth today in Jesus' Name. We don't have silver or gold, but what we have unlocks deadbolts. What we have, makes hundreds of snacks for children in a foreign countries. What we have speaks to a single mom who needs a word from heaven. What we have heals the sick. What we have raises the dead. What we have can change a nation.

What we have can shift our nation. Don't be afraid. Understand who you are. You are the Church of the Living God. You are the Church of the Almighty God. Stand in your authority. Stand in your anointing. Say, "I will be the Church. Not by title only, but by the manifestation in my life, I will be the Church. In this dark hour, I will be the standard God raises up. I will do my job. Lord, I just have to make sure I walk with You; You are all I need."

As we close this chapter, let's pray.

Lord, we cry out for our nation. Our nation is lost, but Lord Your Word says. "Blessed is the nation whose God is the Lord." Father, we come against the anti-Christ spirit that has flooded our nation; we come against it in the Name of Jesus. We tell you Satan and all of your lying spirits, "get your hands off our nation in the Name of Jesus. Get your hands off our young people; get your hands off our children. We rebuke you. The blood of Jesus rebukes you." We rebuke that foul spirit. You will not take our nation. The Remnant is present and we are standing and telling you, not on our watch, not while there's breath in God's people. We recognize who we serve today, and the blood of Jesus rebukes you. Father, we pray for our young people in this nation that have a target on their back, Lord God. I pray God, for a Daniel generation to rise up from in the midst of our young people that love You and that fear You. Protect them from being caught up with the ideologies of this world, Lord God, so that they'll love You and walk with You.

God, make us an unshakeable people, that as everything is shaking around us, we stand, we remain and we don't move. We know who we are and we know who You are. We understand that we don't have silver or gold, but what we have is sufficient. What we have can be shared.

You rule and you reign, God. There's no one else like You, Jesus. Over the heavens and the earth, You reign over it all. Oh, Jesus, we hail You as King of kings and Lord of lords. You are the ruler of the nations, King over heaven and the earth. And so God, as You raise us up, God, we will follow You wherever You go. We will do what You have told us to do. We will say what You tell us to say. May it be Jesus over everything else, God. I pray that You would seal this work in our hearts, God, that as we go forth, we will walk in the authority that You've given us as sons and daughters. Father, we thank you that we will see your kingdom advance on earth just as it is in heaven. In Jesus's Name, Amen.

THE SOUND OF REVIVAL

Family, isn't it great that we can call each other family? If you have given your life to God, we are family. Though we have never met, we are family because we are bought by the same blood. We have the same Father, and we have the same elder brother. It is our honor to be able to gather in His Name.

In this section, I want to address the Pajama Church. The Pajama Church is the culture that was created during the COVID 19 lockdown. I do believe there was a season when the lockdown was necessary, but now we need to get the saints out of their houses and back in the House of God. I can boldly say that the Pajama Church season is over, and we all need to put on our clothes and come to the House of the Lord. The Pajama Church is a church whose attendees seek to compromise what church was meant to be and seek comfort above all else. Let me clarify something for you, nothing about being Christian is comfortable. It's the opposite; being Christian is about being uncomfortable. The Pajama Church is for pancakes, Wi-Fi, and running errands. The Church is supposed to make warriors. We need to get up and stop being comfortable.

We must start getting uncomfortable and return to the House of God. Some people in church say *you should just do what you are comfortable with*. But I am a revivalist, so I will counter that and say you should not do what you are comfortable with! It is not always about you being comfortable. If we wanted to be comfortable, we would not be Christians. Everything about the Gospel was made to make you uncomfortable. That is the purpose of the Gospel. We are not meant to sit in a recliner. We are meant to sit on the edge of our chairs, ready for God to move us at any moment and to do what He wants. So I am calling out the Pajama Church. You must come to Church and be a part of what God is doing in His House.

I have been in church my entire life; I grew up in church. If you are in ministry and you do church well, you wear many hats and can do everything. I have worked in a storefront church, and I have worked in a startup church. I was a youth pastor for eight years in a little Arabic church with 50 adults and over 300 teenagers. And let me tell you, God met us there with great power and great revival. I was also a pastor for 15 years at another church with about 1,500 people. I served as their family life pastor and also served for many years as an executive pastor. I have seen God do great and mighty things. I have been birthed in fire, so I don't know a small God. I don't know a God without power. I don't understand how people walk into church and walk out the same. Something about that makes me undone.

The hope of the world is the Church on fire! Therefore, the Church must get on fire and align with the Spirit of God. I have invested my life in the local church, and I believe the days of the mega-church are over. God is giving the ministry to the local church; to those who have dirty nails; those who are doing the work, and those who are buried in the ground. God is giving the work to them, and I have been called to partner with the local church. I am not here to be a flash in the pan. As a revivalist, I am here to labor with you. I am here to walk with you and see the Kingdom of Jesus Christ advance. That is my purpose.

As I mentioned, God allowed the pandemic to shake all our pretty programs and nice little things. Many of the churches in America are very busy but not very productive. You can see this by looking at the state of our country. If the Church did its job, America would not look the way it does. Somehow the Church started to follow the culture. We are the church! We are not supposed to be a thermometer; we are supposed to be a thermostat. We are supposed to change the culture. We are supposed to speak to the culture. The Church wanted to play nice and did not understand that by not offending people, we offended God. We offended God. So He used the pandemic to remove everything the Church depended on and to bring the basics back to the Church. A Church whose security lies in Him alone and whose first response is prayer no matter what. Thank you, Lord, for loving us enough to strip everything away to get our attention so that we could be the Church you called us to be.

Now we have the post-pandemic church. I know many people want to return to the pre-pandemic church but I do not want to go back there. We have prophetically jumped 50 years in a few months. We are now living the Word that we used to read. We are in the Book of Revelation. We are beginning to walk into things that we have only read about. That gets me really excited because King Jesus wins.

Some think that gracing everything is Jesus. If you read Scripture, Jesus did not grace everything; He told the truth. When He spoke to the woman at the well, He asked her to go and get her husband. When she responded that she didn't have one, Jesus told her she was right; she had five, and the one she was with was not her husband. That does not sound like He sugar-coated anything. When a woman asked Jesus to heal her child. "It is not right to take the children's bread and throw it to the little dogs," was His response. That does not sound very gracious.

Jesus spoke the truth because He loved them. We must speak the truth to those we want to serve because we love them. If I don't speak the truth, I don't love you. Grace is wonderful, but no one grows with just grace. And if it is just truth with no grace, there would be dead bodies everywhere.

The Church in America is very different from churches around the world. How many know that America has now become the mission field of the world? It used to be Africa, but it is not anymore. In America right now, 75% to 80% of the people do not believe in God; do not believe in the Christian God. When I was growing up, everyone knew who Jesus was. Even if they did not attend church, they knew who Jesus was. When I do children's events now, there are children who have never heard the name of Jesus.

It is a different generation; it is a different world. We, as the Church, have to understand our role in it. Our role is to bring transformation. When Jesus left, He gave us a calling. The calling was to go and make disciples. Instead, the Church in America changed the calling to "fill the building." Fill the building. The more people we have attending indicates we are doing our job. However, this is not the case because when push comes to shove, those people will not stand. Why? Because the American Church stopped making disciples, they just filled the building. The American Church changed the Gospel. They stopped talking about sin. They stopped talking about righteousness. They stopped talking about pleasing God, and they stopped talking about discipline.

The Gospel is free. Everything else requires work. The Gospel is free. He gave me salvation, but sanctification is all on me. We performed baptisms without talking about repentance. We invited people to come and be renewed, ignoring the need to die to their old selves. We don't preach this because we are afraid people won't come back, and if they don't come back, we can't fill the building. So, we filled our buildings. We filled all the megachurches. We had a superstar culture of Christianity, and God, in one fell swoop, knocked it all down with COVID. I am not against the megachurch, but it did not do its job. We created this superstar culture and these superstar pastors, and we have watched them fall to the ground one by one.

The Church and the Kingdom look weak and superficial because we were satisfied with buildings being filled instead of lives being changed. We had a superficial experience with no transformation. We were willing to settle for quantity and not quality. God now wants to build the Church His way and make disciples. There is a different group that is rising up as mentioned before. It is a group that has dirt in their nails and is willing to do the work. We may not look as pretty as the superstar culture, but I am not interested in a superstar culture. I am interested in being a disciple. We may not speak as well, but the anointing of God sits on us. God is calling us in this season as His people to recognize that we must

166

bring transformation. What is transformation? It is the Spirit of God bringing change into someone's life, and that will stand the test of time. This transformation will be permanent, not fleeting.

Parents, when asked, will know the difference between their child having a behavior modification versus a transformation. I always tell parents to let their children make mistakes while still in your house. If parents don't, their children will not know how to judge on their own; they will not know how to think clearly, because you have always been the thermostat. That is behavior modification. In your eyes, they will always do what is right, but the second they get on their own, it's all different. It's different because you never allowed them to be transformed; you gave them behavior modification.

I have taught children my whole life. We teach the children to be transformed. Come to Jesus, and learn how to hear Jesus. I conduct chapel services in many schools, and I gather the kids at the altar when I teach. This gives the kids an opportunity to hear from God. And what God is saying to them is profound, so profound.

There are times I share some of my mission experiences during chapel. During one particular Chapel Service, I shared how God performed miraculous things on one of my trips to Africa and how God spared my life. That day, at the chapel, there was a little girl who was not saved, and she gave her life to Jesus. She went home and told her mom about how the pastor's life was saved in Africa. The pandemic was going on at that time, and the single mom could not afford to send the little girl back to the Christian school she had been attending. The little girl insisted, "Jesus told me I'm going back." This unsaved mom wanted to know just how this would happen since there wasn't any money. The little girl persisted, telling her mom that if God could save that pastor's life in Africa, He could make a way for her to return to the Christian school. She prayed over her mother for weeks. She prayed in her house and out loud. On the first day of school, the mom returned her daughter to the private school. The girl's faith was undeniable. God made a way. She won her mother over because she was transformed, not through behavior modification but through true transformation. The Church is fabulous at behavior modification but terrible at transformation. We are terrible at transformation because we lack the power of transformation. We, ourselves, are not stepping out in the way we need to.

The title of this chapter is "The Sound of Revival." We have come to a place in our world where every day, we look at the news and can't believe what is happening. A town school board in New Jersey approved a curriculum to teach kindergarteners about same-sex marriage and all kinds of sexual perversion. Thankfully, a group of parents and Christians hired an attorney. The attorney prepared a report and emailed the report, along with the curriculum, to the Board of Education. The Board of Education's firewalls blocked the curriculum and identified it as pornography. Their own firewalls called it pornography, but they want to teach it to our children?

What we need right now is the greatest move of God's Spirit that has ever happened in our lifetime. We need revival like we have never seen before. We need an outpouring of the Spirit of God that you and I have only read about. The Church needs to come back to life. The Church has been dormant and unproductive for far too long. The Church, which has been sleeping and not doing its job, is now in a position where it needs to come back to life. It needs to begin to see the move and the power of the Holy Spirit. When you see a miracle happen in front of your eyes, there is no doubt that there is a God.

I was in Africa partnering with local pastors doing a kids' crusade in a town that was 99% Muslim. For this crusade, the pastors advised me that we would not get many kids because of the large Muslim population in that town. The parents would not allow them to attend, but I was prepared to minister to whoever would attend, no matter the number of children. They thought maybe 100 kids. So I planned for 200. They laughed and said, "May God give you your faith." So, we began to plan. We rented a field and got some sound equipment, which is quite an act of faith on the mission field. I have eight people as part of my staff, and as we drive to the field, we see hundreds of children. To get ready, we made circles with the kids so we could count them easier. At first, we started with circles of 20. Then we changed it to circles of 30 and then circles of 50. Remember, I only had eight people to help minister, and we had 1,000 children. One thousand Muslim children. We look, and we see about 200 mothers on the side, all wearing their hijabs, and a whole bunch of fathers in the back. I tell my team to march to the field and pray.

As we begin to pray, a man walks over to us and in perfect English, asks me what we are doing. I tell him that we are praying. He says that we need to stop praying. I told him he needed to go. He said, "I'm praying against you." We bind him, he runs off, and we now know that we have hit different ground. The enemy was very upset. As we prepare to start the crusade, the local pastors pull me aside. I could see they were very nervous. They did not expect this. They told us that we needed to finish the crusade by 6 o'clock because that is the time our permit expires. If we go past 6 o'clock, the Muslims can riot against us, and no one will help us. I assured them that we would be done on time. Then they added if I could avoid saying 'Jesus is the Messiah,' because using the word 'Messiah' makes it very clear what we were trying to say. The Muslims will identify it clearly, and they might riot. So if we could avoid saying 'Jesus is the Messiah,' that would be great. "Pastor, I want to honor you. But what would you like me to do if the Lord tells me to say 'Jesus is the Messiah'?" He got quiet and said, "If the Holy Spirit tells you to say it, then say it. But if He doesn't tell you to say it, you don't say it. You can say He is Lord. You can say He is God but don't say He is the Messiah." I agreed.

We finally started the kid's crusade. Kids' crusades in this part of the world are not like ours. This was not two hours but six hours of kids worshiping, dancing, and praising Jesus. Imagine 1,000 children worshiping the Lord. We gave out snacks, candy, and games. It is now time for the salvation message. I have a translator, and I hear the Holy Spirit, clear as a bell, "Tell them I am the Messiah." No problem. I say, "Jesus is the Messiah." The translator looks at me and says, "Really?" I tell him 'yes,' and he translates it, "Jesus is the Messiah." All the pastors that were sitting behind me stopped breathing. Do you know what happened? Nothing.

It was a holy hush. I heard the Lord say again, "Tell them I am the Messiah." So I repeated it. "Jesus is the Messiah." The translator took a deep breath and repeated it. And when I asked how many of them wanted to give their lives to Jesus the Messiah today, every hand went up. Over a thousand children lifted their hands to give their life to Jesus the Messiah. As I looked around, a group of moms had their hands lifted. They took their hijabs off and stepped forward to give their lives to Jesus.

We prayed for over 1,200 people into the Gospel during this crusade. Then we prayed for the sick, and God healed many people. We finished at 5:45 p.m. The pastor was amazed but said they needed to get us out of there immediately because the news was spreading to the villages of what God had done here, and our safety was in danger. They put me in a car with the translator and one of the girls on my team, and we drove off.

In Africa, they block the road with huge rocks when they want to ambush a car. The roads are unpaved, so you can't go around the rocks. You have to stop the car, get out, move the rocks, and that is when the ambush occurs.

As we drove away from the crusade, I felt the Lord tell me we were in trouble. We begin to pray. As we pray, we look up and see the road ahead is completely blocked with rocks, and men are standing on both sides of the road with lanterns. They are there waiting to ambush our car. I could see our driver's hands shaking because he was Muslim and knew what was happening.

I hear the Holy Spirit give me instruction. I turn to the translator and tell him to instruct the driver not to slow down or speed up. He should just keep going straight. The driver questioned the translator, who told him to do what I said. We keep driving. We don't slow down, and we don't speed up as we come to the rocks. As the Lord is my witness, the rocks split right down the middle, right out of our way.

We keep driving. A little further down the road, we saw the road was blocked a second time, and they were waiting for us again. They were determined to get us that day. As we were driving, the driver asked what I wanted him to do. "I already told you, don't slow down, don't speed up, just keep going." As we get to the rocks, they split again right before his eyes. We go a third time, and it is blocked again. This time the driver doesn't even ask me what to do; he just keeps going, and as we come up to the rocks, they split, and we drive home. We are under the umbrella of the Holy Spirit. It was incredible; the most incredible moment of my life, really. We pull up to the hotel. The driver is undone. He is weeping. He turns to me and asks, "Who do you serve? Who do you serve?" And through the translator, we led that driver to the King of kings and the Lord of lords, because with his own eyes, he saw the power of God on display.

We are in a time right now where we need the power of God to show up and be on display to a world that is lost and broken. God still does miracles. God still moves with power. God still heals. And God is looking for people who will believe Him and step out in faith and say, "God, I believe you, even if I look foolish, even if people don't understand. I am going to believe you to split rocks in my life."

When the world sees our God on display, when it sees the power of our God, that is called transformation. They have not seen God because we have not displayed God, but God is ready to be displayed. He is ready to bring out the greatest outpouring we have ever heard. He is looking for people who will live in the sound of revival.

The sound of revival is found in Joel 2:12-24. "Now, therefore," says the Lord, "Turn to Me with all of your heart, with fasting, with weeping, with mourning." So rend your heart, and not your garments; Return to the Lord your God for He is gracious and merciful, slow to anger, and of great kindness; and He relents from doing harm. Who knows if He will turn and relent, and leave a blessing behind Him - a grain offering and a drink offering for the Lord your God? Blow the trumpet in Zion, consecrate a fast, call a sacred assembly; gather the people, sanctify the congregation, assemble the elders, gather the children and the nursing babes: let the bridegroom go out from his chamber, and the bride from her dressing room. Let the priests who minister to the Lord, weep between the porch and the altar; Let them say, "Spare Your people, O Lord, and do not give Your heritage to reproach, that the nations would rule over them. Why should they say among the people, 'Where is their God?'"

"Then the Lord will be zealous for His land, and pity His people. The Lord will answer and say to His people, "Behold, I will send you grain and new wine and oil, and you will be satisfied by them; I will no longer make you a reproach among the nations. But I will remove far from you the northern army, and I will drive him away into a barren and desolate land, with his face toward the eastern sea and his back toward the western sea; His stench will come up, and his foul odor will rise, because he has done monstrous things." Fear not, O land; be glad and rejoice, for the Lord has done marvelous things! Do not be afraid, you beasts of the field; for the open pastures are springing up, and the trees bear its fruit; the fig tree and the vine yield their strength. Be glad then, you children of Zion, and rejoice in the Lord your God; for He has given you the former rain faithfully, and He will cause the rain to come down for you - the former rain, and the latter rain in the first month. The threshing floors shall be full of wheat, and the vats shall overflow with new wine and oil."

That there is called revival. That is revival, when the latter rain and the former rain come together in the first month and fill the land with fruit, vegetation, fresh wine, and fresh oil. There is something called 'promises of God,' and everyone loves them. But there is also something called 'conditional promises,' where something is needed to be done for the promise to be fulfilled. God told Joshua He would give him everywhere his foot would go, but he was not to turn to the right or the left. That is how Joshua received every place his foot marched; by not looking to the right or left. How do we get this? By weeping, mourning, crying out, calling a sacred assembly, gathering the people, and consecrating the house.

That is the sound of revival. Revival does not come because I want it; revival comes because I need it. Revival does not come as a nice gesture. Revival comes because something is dead and needs to come back to life. Revival comes when I look at the Church and ask, "Where is your power? Where is your anointing? Where is your God?" That is how revival comes. When we come to church and refuse to accept the current state of the Church of Jesus Christ, we need to cry out to God and keep crying until He sends rain. We must cry out to God until the heavens open.

People say *I look at my family, knowing things could be better. My son is not serving the Lord, or my daughter is not serving the Lord. I see the sickness in the body of Christ.* As I hear and observe all of this, I know this is not the best God has to offer. God came to give us life and life more abundantly. If we look as bad as the world, why would the world come in? But when the Church rises to be what the Church is supposed to be, the world will be eager to come in. As the Church lifts Him up, He will draw man to Him.

God is looking for people today who are going to be unrelenting in their cry for revival; be unrelenting in their weeping; unrelenting in their fasting; unrelenting in their gathering, and unrelenting in sanctifying themselves. The days of tolerating sin are over.

He is coming back for a Church without a spot or wrinkle. It is time to get to work. It is time to weep between the porch and the altar and cry for a living God to pour His Spirit over us. We need the Church to go back to its original condition. That is what revival is. Lord, what you did in the book of Acts, do it again. Do it in our day. God, I need you. I can't breathe without you. I don't want to be on this planet one more day without the move and the power of Your Spirit. I'm not interested in playing church. I don't want to be comfortable; I want to be on fire. This is what the sound of revival sounds like.

I don't want to look the same as I did five years ago. If we look the same as we did five years ago, something is very wrong. God is looking for people ready to say they don't just want revival but need revival. He is looking for people willing to say I don't want you to move; I need you to move. He is looking for people who can say they can't breathe without His presence and without the outpouring of His Spirit. This world needs the greatest outpouring of the Spirit of God we have ever seen. It needs to see miracles in the streets. It needs to see the power of God showing up because we are about to usher in the second coming of the Lord Jesus Christ. We are preparing the ground. We need to get ourselves in order and begin to weep before God and cry out, "God, send the rain. Send the rain, God. The ground is dry. The trees have no fruit. There is no oil; there is no wine. Send the rain, God. We need you. We need you." The superficial church is over. Only the Remnant with power will survive. Send the rain, God. Send the rain.

Make His Name Famous

Whether preparing a message or writing a book, I go into what I call prep mode. During this time, I don't talk to anyone for a couple of days. I truly believe I need to sit before the Lord before I address His people. I have no right to speak to God's people unless I have sat before the Lord. As I was preparing and fasting for this book, I began to play in my head what God wanted to say.

After sitting and listening to the Lord during this time, I can say that what I have heard from the Lord is that we are in such a pivotal time in history; I can feel it with everything in me! That is what this whole book has been about. The struggle I have is that what I feel is so much bigger than my vocabulary can adequately describe. Since I stepped into the role of Revivalist, people continuously ask how I feel about this season. . My answer is very simple: This is my Esther moment, my kairos moment. *I was made for this season.* All the years in ministry have led to this moment!

I have traveled to preach and have dealt with all the struggles and challenges that come with it. I tell you, if you want to go into the ministry, it is not for the faint of heart! You have to have skin of titanium to work in ministry. You have to learn to live unoffended on a regular basis. You have to learn to live in the consistent habit of forgiveness; that is the ministry and the truth. I have walked through many challenges and feel that every one of them was a building block in preparation for this moment in my life. Every single one of them was building toward this season. All I knew since I was 15 years old was to keep going; keep moving; keep trusting, and to please the Lord.

I am called to remind the Church that we were never called to be a *successful* church. We were called to be a *faithful* church. We want the best lighting and sound to attract a larger crowd. "Hey, how are churches A and B doing that thing? Let's figure that out, and let's copy it." "How did they get so popular?" "How did they get so big?" Can I tell you something? God is not in that. God never called us to be successful; He called us to be faithful! It is not about the numbers. My niece once asked me, "Auntie, do you like preaching to a big crowd or a little crowd?" My response was, "Baby, I like preaching to a hungry crowd." It does not matter if there are five people or 3,000 people. The most important question is, "are they hungry?"

Trying to make people who are not hungry become hungry is an unrealistic task to try and achieve. But the church is seeking success. How do we get more people in? How do we get them to come back? How many gifts can we give them? How many giveaways? How many bouncy houses can we get outside? What guest speaker can we get? God never called us to do that. He said, "If I am lifted up, I will draw them. I don't need you to draw them. Don't do my job. That is the Holy Spirit's job." God said, "I will draw them in. You just lift Me up. You just glorify Me and I will bring them in." This is exactly what happened as I was preaching one Sunday. We had people in the audience that morning who had been driving by and felt pulled to come in. They did not know anything about this church, yet they felt the

Lord pull them in. A couple came in and said, "We saw the cars and thought we should probably go in." They came in, sat the whole service and lifted their hands. Why? Because He was being lifted up. If He is lifted up, He will draw all people. We don't have to strive to bring in people; we just have to lift Him up.

The church got distracted when they started focusing on things like the quality of their sound system. Do you understand that Jesus preached with no sound system? He did not have a nice mic. Two thousand people stood and listened, with no microphone? He did not have a social media presence, He had no Instagram and certainly no hashtag Jesus. He did not have any of those trappings. He simply had the anointing. News of His fame would go ahead of Him because of His anointing. People would hear, *Jesus is coming to town*, and would gather as a result. Knowledge of Jesus' presence was all spread by word of mouth. There was no one taking pictures or tweeting about his coming into town. We were not called to be successful. We were called to be faithful. The Lord said, "faithful over little, and I will make you master over much." As I have walked this life out, that is a lesson that I have learned so deeply. Our life should not be measured by our success but by our faithfulness.

How do I walk before God? How do I honor God? I was fifteen years old when I taught my first Sunday School class. It was a kindergarten class. Naturally, I used my creativity to engage those little ones by using red Jell-O because I knew that on that Sunday morning, I was going to kill all the Egyptians in the Red Sea. During that lesson, I threw the red Jell-O all over the soldiers and the kids went home and told their parents, "God killed the Egyptians with Jell-O."

While the students' interpretation of that bible lesson included Jell-O, I still showed up every day and did my best before the Lord. Whether man liked it or not, whether I got praised or criticized, I still showed up because my heart was set on serving God, and I wanted Him to be pleased. And so God has taken all those lessons and placed me right here at this moment in time. He is looking for people that can be trusted with what is coming. God always puts people He has tested in places He can trust. That is how He works.

I said this before and will repeat it; I will witness the end of the big mega era. They are too big and have become a show instead of a disciple-making church. There is a problem with making everything seeker-friendly. The result of that is a lack of growth. Why? Because you have already dumbed down everything to get them in the door. You have already taken away all non-ear-tickling words like "sin." How can anyone repent if we avoid using words like "sin"? How can anyone be baptized without repentance? The message is to lay down your old life, with all its sinful ways and come up as a new person; that is the message. That sincere transformation brings about a different way of doing church, and I am grateful for it.

There was a prophet with a word at the beginning of 2022, and it witnessed to my heart. I want to share that word with you today. He saw a card game happening; it was a poker game. And he saw the devil sitting at the head of the table, and there were six seats. Five well-dressed men came and sat down to play. I don't know much about cards so let's say they put down two pairs of each toward the devil. The devil laughed and put down two aces. The five men bowed their heads and walked off because they had lost.

But there was a man that was coming late to the party. He was dirty. He had dirt in his fingernails and mud on his face. He came running in and on his shirt was the word "Remnant." He sits down and they begin to play. The enemy automatically puts down his aces, and the man looks up, smiles, and pulls out a royal flush. The Lord was saying at that moment, "I am not giving this revival to the ones that look pretty and have not been in the trenches. I am giving it to the ones that have been in the trenches with the dirty nails; the ones that have been doing Kingdom work and have been faithful in their calling. The ones doing what I have called them to do in this hour and in this place. I am not giving this revival to the ones who just want to look fancy but to those who have done the work. Those people I have equipped with a royal flush. I have given them everything they need to work in this hour and be My people." I believe that word because I have seen those dirty nails for years. I have seen them in the spirit. I have seen the people that no one would invite to the party and those who don't look like they belong.

When I remember this prophet's word, I think of King David and how God saw his heart when no one else did. Samuel asked David's father the funniest question in Scripture, "Don't you have any more sons?" Didn't he say to bring all your sons? But his own father did not even think he was worthy! In answering Samuel, he said, "Yes, I have one son, but it can't be him. He is just a kid." But Samuel would not continue until the father brought the son in. The second David walks in, Samuel says, "That is the one."

As I watch this season unfold, I see His people and pastors with the dirty nails. These people have been putting in work and making disciples. This is the call. It is not to make a big building but to make disciples. It is not to make a big ministry but to make disciples; make disciples, not converts. It is not about how many hands get lifted but how many people get plugged in and begin to grow. The evangelist Reinhard Bonnke is the greatest evangelist in the history of Christianity. He recently passed in 2021 and left a tremendous legacy. His life was marked with three million disciples, three million!

The man that took over his ministry made a distinction. He said, "We did not say 'converts' because we do not count every hand lifted. We take the decision cards and connect these people to a church. When we get reports that they are connected with that church, that is when we count them." He continued. "Hands? That would be in the billions because he preached all over Africa: hands would be in the billions. Disciples? Three million; that is when we count them." And that family is what we are called to do. Reinhard Bonnke did not own a building because it is not about a building. We are not here to build a building. I feel in my spirit that if you are reading this book, you were also made for this moment. You have walked through circumstances that have made you who you are today, and I pray you say, *God I'm ready. I'm ready. I'm ready to be what You have called me to be.*

The time we are in right now is not very different from the time in which Habakkuk lived. I love Habakkuk, but we do not know a lot about Habakkuk. We know he was a prophet, and we know he was a frustrated prophet. In some ways he was like Jonah; very frustrated. Prophets are frustrated because they can see beyond what is before them. They can see something and want it now. They do not understand why people are spiritually blind because they can see it. So there is frustration with that. I, too, was like that when working with people. I could see the potential in them that they could not. I would say to them, "Hey, don't you see it? Because I see it!" And so here is Habakkuk, frustrated because he is watching evil unfold. He is watching darkness and watching the Chaldeans and the Assyrians cover the people of Israel. It seems to be that God is silent.

The whole book of Habakkuk is a dialogue between God and Habakkuk. In his frustration, Habakkuk asks, "God, why are you silent? Why are you silent? God, why have you not responded yet?" Habakkuk 1:2-4 says, "O Lord, how long shall I cry, And you do not hear? Even cry out to You, "Violence!" And You will not save. Why do You show me iniquity, And cause me to see trouble? For plundering and violence are before me; There is strife, and contention arises. Therefore, the law is powerless, And justice never goes forth. For the wicked surround the righteous, Therefore perverse judgment proceeds."

So what is Habakkuk saying? He is saying, *God, why are you not responding? Everything is evil around me. How long will I cry out to You, God? And You do not answer? It is evil. There is strife. There is hatred. Even the law itself is powerless because the judges are corrupt. Why are You not answering God?* Was this written today? It certainly sounds like it could be written today. In frustration, Habakkuk asks, "God, where are You?" Have you ever wondered, "God, why are You being silent at this moment? Why are You not roaring at this moment, God?" As I've mentioned before, God has two speeds: "pause" or "run."

At this moment, God is "paused" in Habakkuk's mind. He feels like God is not moving. *Can't God see that the judges are perverse?*

There is contempt, strife, and hatred. The Assyrians and the Chaldean surround us and are unfair to us. Yet God still seems silent to him. But then God begins to answer. His answer is found in Habakkuk 2:1-4. "Then the Lord answered me and said: Write the vision And make it plain on tablets, That he may run who reads it. For the vision is yet for an appointed time; But at the end it will speak, and it will not lie. Though it tarries, wait for it; Because it will surely come, It will not tarry. Behold the proud, His soul is not upright in him; But the just shall live by his faith."

This is the first time we see the verse, "The just shall live by faith," in Scripture. But we see it again in The New Testament. God answers Habakkuk by telling him that he is to write it down on the tablet, and it will come to pass. It is going tarry, but it will surely come to pass. God assures Habakkuk that this is the moment He is in and that He has not forgotten His people. The wicked will be lost, but the just will learn to live by faith. He instructs Habakkuk to write down His words and read them. Why? So when we read it, we can run! Run towards what? Run towards what we are reading. The just that live by faith are not running towards what they can see in the physical. They are running towards what they can see in the Heavens. They are not running towards earthly things.

Take my story, for example. Every time I go up for prayer, I expect my chronic cough to be gone. I pray it is gone every day because I already see myself without it. I say, "You have to go" daily because my faith is in God, not here. God is saying here the just shall live by faith. Write it on the tablet so you can remember and look at it daily. So you can see it and run towards it. Don't run towards what you are looking at in the physical; run towards what God is instructing you to write; run towards what God is saying. And then Habakkuk writes this verse that we repeat all the time, "the just shall live by faith." Habakkuk takes this word in and he begins to pray differently. He begins to pray prophetically because he is doing what the Lord is telling him to do at that moment. And now, his dialogue changes, and he begins to realize something. He realizes that his frustration has no earthly solution. There is no earthly solution for what he is dealing with. It is the same for us today. What we are dealing with has no earthly solution. No lawmaker or president will have the solution we need. There is no earthly solution for what we are living through.

The solution people come up with is *we just have to make a better way. We just have to make people love each other more. We have to come up with a different plan to try and build some type of happy place.* Let me tell you, Adam and Eve were in utopia when they fell. There was no better place than the Garden of Eden, and they still chose to sin. So it is not about getting to a better place. It is not about you and I holding hands and singing "We Are The World." That is not the solution.

It is not about a law. No law changes racism, and no law changes hatred. Take India, for example. Did you know that in the 1970s, the caste system was outlawed? The caste system existed in some form in India for over 3,000 years. It divided people into five classes or castes. The aristocrats were in the first caste, and the fifth caste were called the untouchables. And that is literally what they were, untouchable. I traveled to India in 2011, and all I saw was the caste system on display, even though it had been outlawed decades ago. Do you know why? Because laws do not change anyone's heart. The Kingdom changes people's hearts. Only the Kingdom can change the heart of a man.

As Habakkuk realized there was no earthly solution, we, too, must realize there is no earthly solution. As Habakkuk begins to pray prophetically, he realizes that his solution has to come from the heavens and that the Lord Himself is the solution. The only thing that will change a heart is the Lord Himself. In Habakkuk 3:2, we see how Habakkuk then prays, "Lord, I have heard of your fame; I stand in awe of your deeds, Lord. Repeat them in our day, in our time, make them known." Again. "Lord, I have heard of your fame; I stand in awe of your deeds, Lord. Repeat them in our day." That begins to be the echo of the Book of Habakkuk.

What deeds are Habakkuk talking about? He is talking about when Israel left Egypt. He is talking about the Red Sea parting. He is talking about the manna that poured down from heaven. He is talking about the quail coming down from the skies. He is talking about the Jericho walls falling down. He is talking about the parting of the Jordan River.

He says, *Lord, I have heard what you used to do. I heard how you rescued my people before. I heard about the Red Sea. I heard how you drowned the entire Egyptian army in the Red Sea. Lord, I know what you've done. I've heard it. I've heard it.* He could have easily said my grandmother told me the stories. He could have easily said that he read about them because no one had lived those stories at that time. They were now historical. But Habukkuk did not want historical stories. He wanted his own story! *I want you to renew Your fame in our day, God. I want You to make Your Name known.*

The mission of my ministry is to Make the Name of Jesus Famous. And this is where the church has strayed. The church has clearly shown that it wants to make the name of its individual church famous. As the Lord is my witness, I do not want anybody to remember my name. I'd rather they say, *I saw Jesus through her, and when I met her, I felt Jesus. My name is irrelevant.* All that matters is that Jesus be elevated and that I make the Name of Jesus famous. Yet here we have people who desire mausoleums for their name or their church name, which is all wrong. Habakkuk begins to pray this out, "Lord, renew Your fame." What he really is saying is, *We need a miracle. We need Your power, God. We need You to show up the way You show up. God, we need You to see the darkness around us and respond with the supernatural because what is in the natural is not enough.* God will always bring you to that place so you can cry out to Him.

When I started in ministry, I was given a church as my first assignment. I thought, "Lord help me; I'm being handed a church nobody wants!" Seasoned pastors responded by saying, "Oh, no, we're good," and here I was, a kid fresh out of Bible school. But the Lord said, "Take it." And I said, "What? Take it? Nobody else wants it. It's a hard church." But in obedience, I took it. That night I had a dream that I was buying shoes. I walked into this shoe store and the shoes were like massive clown shoes. I said, "Lord, I don't want these shoes." He said, "Buy them." So I bought them. I said, "Lord, I can't walk in these things." He said, "Put them on." So I put them on and I looked ridiculous. I kept falling and trying to grab onto things. I am asking God, "Lord, what is this?" He said, "Lean on me." As I leaned on Him, I began to walk. And as I began to walk my foot got steady. I began to walk some more, and my footing felt more secure. I said, "Lord, what is this?" He said, "It is the ministry. If your foot can fit it, you do not need Me. I will always give you more so that you will always lean on Me. I will always make it bigger than you so that you need Me. If it fits you, why would you need Me? It is always going to be bigger." God has put us in a place that is significantly bigger than us. We can all look at what is going on and say, *God, this is massive. It is bigger than us.* But I promise it is not bigger than Him.

It is not bigger than Him. So why did He put us in this place? He put us in this place to cry out as Habakkuk did. *Lord, renew Your fame in our day. You did it for Israel. You did it in the Book of Acts. Now do it again. Do it now. Respond, God, now. Renew Your fame in our day. Bring the miraculous move of Your spirit in this time. Family,* nothing changes the equation like the power of the living God, nothing.

I was having dinner with my mom one night. Being a true New Yorker, if something is wrong with the dinner, I send it back. That is just what New Yorkers do! When my food came, it was wrong, but I was still very polite to the waitress. They kept getting my order wrong - three times! Finally, the waitress says, "You're being so nice. Thank you so much." I said, "No, we're all good. We're fine." And as I finished, I felt the Lord. I knew I was supposed to pray for her. I said, "Listen, I'm a pastor. I would love to pray for you. Can I pray for you before I go?" And she says, "Yes, please." I said, "Okay, what can I pray for?" She gave me a list. I thought to myself, "oh, we are going to be here for a while." But I took her hand and began to pray for her list. As I prayed, the Lord gave me a prophetic word for her. And as I gave her the word, she tightened her grip on my hand, and I could feel her beginning to tremble. As I opened my eyes, I looked at her. She was sobbing and said, "You don't know what just happened to me. And I actually can't talk." So she kissed her fingers and kissed my cheek. I responded, "I'm going to wait here till you come back because I want to talk to you." She said, "Okay." She ran, wiped her face, came back, and said nothing. She just hugged me and cried in my arms. God met her in the middle of this restaurant. I could have said a million words. It would not have mattered as much as what the Holy Spirit said to her. What she had going on in her life was bigger than her but not bigger than our God!

That there is God renewing His fame in our day. Nothing changes the equation like the power of a Living God. And here, it is as though Habakkuk is saying, *God, what I'm looking at is much bigger than me, but it is not bigger than You. So God, step in with the same force You used when You took Your people out of Egypt, the force that parted the Red Sea, God. Move on our behalf.* And it came from this cry out of his belly, out of his heart, saying, *God, renew Your fame in our day, God. Make Your deeds known. Make Your Name famous. Make Your Name famous, God. In this time, God, let them see You. Let them have no explanation except to worship a Living God. Let them have no answer.*

Remember the testimony about my lungs? Every time I see The Dr, he asks, "How are the lungs?" And I say, "You know how they are. They are miraculous. Wasn't that your word?" That is God. He healed me from one day to the next. He flips the equation. And we are in a place right now where our cry has to be this cry, "God, renew Your fame in our day. Make Yourself known. Let Your deeds be evident, God. Begin to move in power."

We are the conduit for what God wants to do on earth. We are the ones that lay hands. He put the anointing in us. It comes very simply, "Signs and wonders follow them that believe." So what does that mean? There is a motion to it. We are not sitting still saying, "God use me." We are moving and saying, "God use me." We are not sitting in our chairs saying, "God, whenever you are ready." No. God said, *I am ready; start moving. I have been ready to start moving. I am not going to lift your hand; I am not going to open your mouth. I have been ready to start moving. Start being My church. Start moving up.* And if you make a mistake, make a mistake. What is the worst thing that can happen? You pray for somebody?

Doing something in faith is better than doing nothing in fear. Doing something in faith is significantly better than doing nothing in fear. Fear will keep you in that seat for the rest of your life. Fear will trap you there till Jesus returns. No, if you want His fame to be known, you have to start moving, Child of God, and He will give you the increase; He will give you the anointing, and He will give you the faith. You want to pray for the sick, but you are not willing to pray for a headache? You have to start moving. You have to start somewhere. *I want to lay hands on cancer.* Great, let's start with a headache. You have to kill a lion and a bear before you kill Goliath. You have to start somewhere.

I have children who pray over the sick all the time. Why? Because I want them to build faith. I say, "Hey boys and girls, come here. The pastor has a headache. Can you pray for me?" And they pray for me. This is what they do, "Lord, touch her, heal her. Amen. You're better, right?" I better say "Yes." They believe. Then I watch them go home to their parents, and their parents tell me, "My daughter prayed for my ankle, and God healed it." "My daughter prayed for my husband's back." Faith grows. How does God renew His fame? He renews it through His Church, as His church begins to operate in the gifts. As we step out of what is comfortable, we begin to take chances for God to use us.

What happened to Jonathan was similar to that. Jonathan, the son of Saul, was walking with his armor-bearer and saw a garrison of the Philistine armies. A garrison could have been between 20 to 50 soldiers. But it was only the two of them against this garrison. Jonathan turned to his armor-bearer, saying, "Hey, do you want to take them?" And his armor-bearer looked at him and said, "Do what's in your heart? I'll follow you." Maybe God has also given us this opportunity. Maybe God has put things in our hands. Let us seize the moment." The story goes on to say that Jonathan and his armor-bearer went out and took out the Philistines.

That is how we have to begin to walk. Maybe there is an opportunity here. Let's seize the moment. Let's drop the seed. Let's reach out. "Is your leg hurting? Can I pray for you?" They'll say, Oh, you want to pray for me? Come, let me just put my hands on you and pray. Is that okay?" Let them say no; that's okay. That's on them. How does the church advance? That is how it advances; God begins to move through his people as they begin to trust Him. Move out and say, "Maybe God has put this in my hands. Maybe this soul right here is for me to harvest. Maybe this is the opportunity I need to seize."

I was having dinner in Hershey Park with some friends one day. The waitress came by, and she looked really sad. As I looked at her hand, I saw she had a tattoo of the tree of life on her wrist. I've only known people that get this tattoo in memory of someone who died. So I ask, "Hey, Tina, who died?" She responds, "oh, you know?" I say, "I know about the tattoo." She says, "My brother, my brother died." And I instantly say, "Your baby brother." She then responds, "How did you know that?" I say, "I'm not really sure. Maybe something in your tone." She replies, "Yes, my baby brother." I saw another tattoo, and it was a date. So I ask, "And the number on your arm, what is that?" "It's my mom." she says, "She passed too? Yeah, they went within a year of each other." I asked her if she had any family left. She replied, "I don't have anybody." I said, "I'm so sorry." She said, "Yeah," and started to tear up. I said, "It must be incredibly lonely. I'm so sorry." "It's kind of hard to breathe every day." I said, "Well, you know, God wants you to know that He hasn't forgotten you." "Well, I feel very forgotten." My response was, "Well, you are kind of pretty special because six pastors are sitting at this table, and God has stopped our lunch to minister to you. So you are pretty special to God." Surprised, she says, "You're all pastors." I said, "Yes, we will all pray for you if you let us." "I... I think I'd like that," was her response. We all got around her as she wept, and we ministered to our waitress right there.

She walked away, beaming. She kept bringing us extra food. I was like," Honey, we don't need any. We're good. Please stop bringing us Hershey chocolate bars, please." But she didn't know how to show gratitude. We gave her a Bible; actually, one of the pastors gave away her own Bible. "You can have mine," she told the waitress. "It's already highlighted for you. It has everything you need in it." We found a church nearby for her. That is how He makes His Name known. That is how He renews His deeds in our time. It is when the church begins to take the anointing that is in us and begins to move out with it. We are not supposed to bring the anointing just into the house of God. We are supposed to unleash the anointing out there everywhere we go. The Kingdom of Jesus Christ should advance everywhere we step out. Why? Because a Child of God is present. I repeat, because a Child of God is present. The circumstance should shift every time we walk into something.

We, unfortunately, are sometimes oblivious to our authority. We have no idea who we are. While ministering in a church, I was praying for a girl who had schizophrenia. And as I was praying for her, the girl told me that this was the first time in her life she felt clear. "My mind feels clear," she said. And as I am praying for her, there's another demon-possessed girl beside her. I cannot pray for her yet because I am still praying for the other girl. But this demon-possessed person keeps saying to me, "Stop praying. Stop praying." I responded, "I'm going to deal with you in a minute." But she was getting louder, so I turned around and said, "Be quiet. Be quiet." She then takes off running to the back of the church, but the people in the church stop her. I ask them just to hold her there, and I will be there in a minute. When I finished praying, I went to the back, and saw that the team had her and they were praying over her. There is one woman on the team who was fierce in her prayers. While I felt they had the situation in hand, this team member said, "No no. We don't know how to do this." I said, "No. But you're going to figure it out. I'm going to be in the front. I have all those people to pray for, so you guys have to do this. I'm right down there. If you need me, just give a thumbs down and I'll come." Questioning, she asked, "So what am I doing?" I said, "You are standing in your authority. This demon has to bow. It has no choice." So they surround the girl and continue to pray. I went to the front and continued to pray for people. I kept looking at the team in the back to ensure they were all right. Twenty minutes later, that girl was free.

Two years later, I was at another church telling this story and a young lady came up to me. I did not recognize her. She said to me, "Hey, do you remember me?" "Your face looks familiar, but I'm not sure." "I'm the girl you are talking about in the story." I told her that she looked completely different. She said, "I've been free for two years. I'm really sorry I messed up the service." I said, "Baby girl, you are the reason that I get up in the morning. It is to see people like you transformed. You did not mess up the service. You made the service. Your deliverance made the service. If God gathered us together for your deliverance, blessed be the Name of the Lord. Blessed be the Name of the Lord."

We, as the church, need to understand that we are to be unleashed in the world. We are to invade what is going on. The Kingdom should advance as we walk, and as we do that, His fame will be made known everywhere we go. We need to begin to pray, "Lord, make Your Name known, renew Your deeds in our day, God. I don't want to hear about what you did. I want to live in what you are doing. I don't want to hear about what you did. That was great for Peter, but I am not Peter. That was great for Moses, but I am not Moses. I want Marsha's stories. I want my stories. I love his stories, but he's gone. I want mine. Where are my stories?" Do you know how we change a generation that is coming after us? Stop telling them about what God used to do. Tell them about what God is doing. Tell them what God is doing now.

When my nephews or niece see these things, they don't know what to do, but I see it reflected in how they pray later. They will say, "Aunt Marsha, that person is sick. Go pray for them." I tell them, "No, no. We will go pray for them. Not me. We will pray together." Sometimes they bring their friends. "Aunt Marsha, she's having problems; talk to her." Why? Because they see something and understand it is not about a God that *used to* do things. It is about a God that *is* doing things. He is a God that is doing things today. And God is looking for a people today that say, "God, I want to be a conduit of Your spirit. I want you to renew Your work today. I want Your deeds to be made known. I want Your Name to be made famous through my life. I will not allow everyone else to make Your Name famous and I just sit here like a bump on a log. No, I am moving. I am moving, God. And I am going to let Your Name be known through my life. As Habakkuk began to pray this out prophetically, pray this out too. "This is my cry. God renew Your fame in my day, God. Make Your Name known. Make Your Name known."

There is something about the Name of Jesus that should rattle everything around it. You can say Muhammad all day, and no one gets rattled. No one even gets offended. Go up to someone and tell them that Muhammad loves you. Then tell them Jesus loves you. You get one or two reactions. Why? Because even the unbeliever knows there is power in the Name of Jesus. Even atheists know there is power in the Name of Jesus. Why does it bother them so much? Why does it shake them so much? Tell them Buddha loves you. See if there is a response. They will laugh. Tell them Jesus loves you, and their response is, "Don't say that to me." Why? Why does that bother them so much? Because every man innately in his heart knows that Jesus is the truth. Whether they accept it or not is on them. But every man in his heart knows that He is the Lord. And so, as the church, we must begin to respond to what we see around us. By beginning to be conduits of the Spirit of God and allowing His Name to move through us. As we move, the

Kingdom should advance wherever we go. Everywhere we step into; your job, Costco, etc. It doesn't matter where you go.

Are you advancing the Kingdom? It should be happening wherever we go. Are you the people of God? As we move, the Kingdom should advance. His Name should be made famous through our lives. And I challenge you to begin to pray this out. "God, every day, every day, God, make Your Name known. Renew Your fame in my day. Let my children and the children around me see a God doing mighty things."

I was closing on a new house in 2017 and preparing to move in. I had a Vacation Bible School that I was running simultaneously (apparently, God loves to move during my VBS week). As I mentioned earlier, I used to lead a VBS for a thousand children with 300 volunteers. We were jam-packed with work. The closing on my house got mixed up and ended up being the first day of the VBS. Let's do a closing; why not? So I'm trying to pack, move, shift, and everything else. I was selling one house and buying another. I had a young girl, Raquel, whom I call my niece, staying with me. She was at Bible School at the time. She was hanging out with me when I got a call from my realtor. Everything went south. The paperwork is not in, and we are not going to be able to move tomorrow. I told Michelle, my realtor, "The Lord told me I am moving tomorrow." Michelle, who is a Christian, says to me, "So what am I supposed to do with that now? I am telling you that this is what is happening." I said, "You do your job. I do mine. That's what we do. You do everything you're supposed to do on your side. And I'm going to do everything I'm supposed to do on my side, deal"? And she says, "Yes!"

So Raquel says (she calls me auntie,) "Auntie, so we're not moving?" I said, "No, we are moving. Let's finish packing." She replied, "But the realtor said the paperwork is not ready." My response was, "Raquel, God said we are moving tomorrow. Let's do our job." So we finished packing and got ready. We actually slept in sleeping bags because everything was packed up. The moving truck shows up. They take my whole house. Raquel says," Auntie, we're homeless." "We're not homeless, Raquel. God already spoke."

The closing was set for 5 o'clock. At 4:55 my realtor calls, and she's weeping. "I don't know how this happened. Heaven and earth moved. This doesn't happen; my whole office is crying." I said, "Does that mean I'm closing?" She says, "You have 10 minutes. Get here." I'm like, "OK." "Raquel, you're in charge of everything," and I ran out." She asks, "Auntie, we're moving?" I said, "We're moving." Her response was, "I'm never going to doubt God again. I'm never going to doubt God again." As time passed, I watched her as she tried to get her finances for college. And she began to lean into that testimony, saying, "No, no. You made a way for my Auntie. You are going to make a way for me." God kept blessing her and blessing her.

She would share the story with her friends and tell them not to worry about their tuition because of what happened to her Pastor. "It really happened. I was there and witnessed it with my own eyes." That is how you build a generation. That is how you build a people. You let them see the deeds of our God. You let them see the faithfulness of our God. Sometimes we want to give them the rules or a manual to follow. Don't give them rules; show them who He is. So when they fall in love with Jesus, they won't have a taste for the world. They won't have an appetite for it. When they see for themselves a God that is moving and living and breathing in their life, it's all good from there. I want us to begin to pray this verse out as a Church. And I want you to begin to pray it out daily in your life. "Lord, I've heard of Your fame. I stand in awe of Your deeds. Lord, renew them in our day. In our time, make them known, make them known." I challenge you, people of God, to begin to move in this verse daily. Lord, use me to make Your Name known. I've heard of Your fame. I know of Your deeds. Renew them in our day."

Pray this with me:

Living God, we bless You. Worthy is Your Name, King Jesus. Lord, we love the stories that we read in the Old Testament. We love the Book of Acts. But Lord, our prayer today is the same as Habakkuk. Renew Your fame in our day, Lord God. Let Your deeds be known. We stand in awe of what You have done, Lord God, but we want to see what you will do in our time. We stand in awe of the testimonies, Lord God, but we want our own testimonies. We want our own stories. God, we bless You. We recognize that what is in front of us is bigger than us, Lord God. And it needs a miraculous response.

There is no earthly response for the evil that has encamped around us, Lord God. The same as when Habakkuk saw the Chaldeans and the Assyrians surround his people and said, it is corrupt, God; it is evil. The judges are powerless. The laws are useless. There is no hope in the arm of flesh. There is no deliverance in the arm of flesh. Deliverance only comes from You, God. And Lord, we look at our legal system. We look at our government, Lord God. We look at our school system. We look at all the things around us. They are corrupt, God. We see evil. We

198

see the enemy big and bold. And Lord, we must have a supernatural response to what is happening. We want to be Your people, Lord God. We want Your Kingdom to advance. We recognize God that the only response is a response from heaven. We need a supernatural response, God.

Renew Your fame in our day, my God. Send revival. Send revival, Lord God. Make us a people of faith and courage. Make us a people of boldness. Father, make us fearless in this hour. Make us fearless, God. Cause us to fear no man. Cause us to fear only You. My God, cause us to fear only You. We say Yes now, God. We say Yes, God. We will be your conduits, God. We say Yes, God. We say Yes, God.

We recognize that signs and wonders follow those that believe, Lord God. We receive that Word, and we refuse to sit and wait for You to move us, Lord God. We refuse to sit God and say, "Whenever you are ready, God, let me know." You already let us know God. You already let us know.

Use us, God, to advance Your Kingdom. Use us, God, to make Your Name famous on this earth. Use us, God, for people to be delivered and set free. Father, cause deliverance to happen in Costco. Cause deliverance to happen in ShopRite: Lord God, at our workplaces, at the gas station, on vacation, in an airplane, in an Uber; God, wherever we go. Wherever Your church goes, let Your Kingdom advance. Let Your Kingdom advance. Father, we are sitting waiting for the gifts, but the gifts are not for those who are sitting. The gifts are for those that are moving. You are not going to give us gifts as we sit. You are going to give us gifts as we move out. May we understand that signs and wonders, words of knowledge, healing, and deliverance come in motion. God, there must be a supernatural response to what is in front of us. The enemy has come for our generation, but we will STAND!:

Then say this to Satan out loud:

Satan, we're telling you, Not on our watch, not on our watch. We will not allow you to have them. The Church of Jesus Christ stands in its place, and the blood of Jesus rebukes you today. You are a lying spirit. We bind you now. You will not have this generation. We build a hedge of protection around them in the Name of Jesus.

We build a hedge of fire around them; you will not have them. They will be a righteous generation; they will be a Daniel generation. They will rise up from among them and look you in the face and will not fear you. They will be a generation filled with signs and wonders. They will be a generation that knows what it is to live for the King of kings and the Lord of lords. They will be holy. They will be righteous, and they will be anointed. We are saying No to you; you cannot have them. We don't care what you build around them; God is greater.

Then say out loud to The Lord:

And Father, we have the authority to stand for the generations in all the churches and in all the schools. This is the authority God has given His Church.

And so, Father, we pray that You would shut down the agenda of darkness right now. Satan, we cancel your assignments in the Name of Jesus. Father, we pray for righteousness to rise up in School Board Councils; in the White House; in government; in Senate houses, Lord God. Righteous men and women, Lord God, who are willing to say, "No way, no way." We will not allow you to do this. We pray for darkness to be exposed and removed in the Name of Jesus. Father, it is not enough to expose it: remove it. God and raise up righteousness in its place. Let there be a revival among our students, our children, and our young people, Lord God.

Pray today and every day for the courage to STAND! It is time for the Remnant Church to arise!

ABOUT THE AUTHOR

REVIVALIST MARSHA MANSOUR emigrated from Egypt to the United States with her family at the age of three. She is a Zion Bible Institute graduate and the first Egyptian female ordained minister of the Assemblies of God on the East Coast. Revivalist Marsha is an anointed conference and convention speaker and has served in a pastoral capacity for over two decades. She has prepared leaders and ministries everywhere she has served.

She is also a four-time best-selling author! Her first book, titled *The Courage to Live*, is filled with personal testimonies of God's power and faithfulness, and her second book, *The Courage to Lead*, truly speaks to the heart of every leader. In addition, she has released two devotionals entitled *60 Days of Fresh Manna* and *60 More Days of Fresh Manna*, inspired by her very sought-after vlog titled Monday Manna. She also hosts an international online prayer meeting!

Revivalist Marsha resigned from her pastoral position to pursue the call of God to be a full-time Revivalist! Her passion is to see the church walk in God's Fullness! She is an igniter for the kingdom and has committed her life to see the church be the Church that Jesus built!

LETS STAY CONNECTED!

Facebook

- @revmarsham
- fb.com/revmarsham
- YT.com/MarshaMansour
- www.marshamansour.com

Marsha Mansour Ministries

To stay up-to-date with our ministry and all services, download our app

(Available in all App Stores)

Learn more at
www.marshamansour.com

Made in the USA
Columbia, SC
17 February 2023

12390721R00120